The BALLPARKS

The BALLPARKS

Bill Shannon and George Kalinsky

with a Foreword by Monte Irvin

HAWTHORN BOOKS, INC.
Publishers/New York

Library of Congress Catalog Card Number: 75-5035
ISBN: 0–8015–0490–2
1 2 3 4 5 6 7 8 9 10

Contents

357

Foreword

To me, one of the most impressive things about making it to the major leagues as a ballplayer is your first time in a big league park. The atmosphere and surroundings are so different from any other ballpark you might ever have played in before. The really important thing, of course, is being there as a player, a member of the team. But things begin to happen to you when you come within sight of the park for the first time. It's a little unreal, difficult to describe, but the sensation is not unlike that first time you go to a ball game as a kid.

The sheer size of big league ballparks is awesome, especially to a young player whose experience is limited to high school, college, or the minor league parks—or a guy like me who, before the days of Jackie Robinson, played in some strange places in what were then called the Negro Leagues. We played in a big league park on a rare occasion, for an all-star game or special exhibition; but that was not really like being a big leaguer and belonging on that field, knowing you were going to come back again tomorrow and the day after.

In this book, Bill Shannon's words and George Kalinsky's artistry have captured many feelings. The big league ballpark works on different levels, naturally, for the player, the fan, the beer vendor, and so forth. It means something different to everyone attending a ball game. But it was especially in the early post-World War II era, when television first started bringing the famous old parks into the livingroom, that the Polo Grounds, Ebbets Field, Crosley Field, and all the other parks of the time really became part of America. Even though the early telecasts were not in color, a feeling of color was transmitted across the screen of the television by these great old buildings.

I was a Giant, so of course the Polo Grounds will always be a special place for me. There was no ballpark like it, then or now. It had a contour all its own. That odd shape influenced every game played there and also placed the fans closest to the action in areas where they were still far away.

Ebbets Field was another special place of that time. It, too, had its oddities in construction, but the atmosphere was what made it special. Again, for a Giant that feeling had a very intense meaning. When you walked onto the grass at Brooklyn in your gray flannel road uniform with NEW YORK printed across its front, the feeling of hatred focused at you was so thick you could cut it with a knife. Playing against the Dodgers at Ebbets Field was always a special challenge and one I rather enjoyed, although some of my teammates over the years got a little unnerved by it.

Today's ballparks still have their unique feeling. There is an ambience in a ballpark that simply doesn't exist anywhere else, ever. For a few hours, a little piece of America all comes together. Fans who don't know each other and may never meet again are all pulling for something in common, sharing a goal, an interest, and a time of fun and excitement. I imagine that the same feeling was present in the old, old parks in baseball's early days, just as it was in my time as a player—and as it is now, because it is that indefinable mixture of baseball, its players and fans, and the ballpark which has always produced it.

Ballparks in America are something more than concrete and steel; they have an extra dimension, like rare old historic buildings. If you walk into the Lincoln Memorial in Washington, you can almost hear the great president's voice—or at least what you imagine as his voice. I have always felt that same feeling in a ballpark. Even an empty ballpark can produce this effect. Your mind does the work of the players, fans, umpires, and ushers. It creates the scene and you can almost hear the crack of the bat against the ball. In those old ballparks that still survive, like Fenway Park, White Sox Park, Tiger Stadium, and Wrigley Field, the recollection of the great players and famous stories come back just the way you heard them from your father or over the radio in your childhood. The newer ballparks, too, are building a history of their own like that every day a game is played in them. Dodger Stadium is only fourteen years old, but it already has a rich collection of memories. Today's game becomes tomorrow's nostalgia for each generation.

In the following pages the entire history of ballparks in the major leagues is unfolded. But in addition, for me, the feeling associated with many of the parks is renewed and refreshed. That is the greatness of baseball and the charm of this work. It is more than a preservation of history; it is an experience that brings to life a set of memories that will vary for each reader.

MONTE IRVIN
*Assistant to the
Commissioner of Baseball*

Preface

When we go to a ballgame, we are really going to a ballpark. Often, that's even what we *say* we are going to do. The ballpark, per se, is not the reason for the going, since few of us go to one regularly when no games are being played. But the ballpark is an integral part of American life. The buildings themselves are part of the total picture of a ballgame. The same game is played differently in different parks.

Even apart from the events presented within them, ballparks have developed interesting histories. They have moved through several phases and are now emerging from another, an orgy of publicly financed stadium construction. Governmental involvement in America's architecture appears inevitably to produce uninspired uniformity and dulling sameness. It has largely done so with ballparks. To justify huge public expenditures, public officials created the oval or circular "all-purpose" ballpark, which theoretically caters to all outdoor sporting needs in the community. In reality, it generally caters to none well and to all with mediocrity. Publicly financed activity has given us ballparks without personalities.

In large measure, that is what this book is about—the personalities of ballparks. Despite the best efforts of planners, even today's newest parks still have their own small idiosyncrasies, weather factors, hitting backgrounds, playing surfaces, and wind currents, all varying slightly.

Without doubt, the best of the governmental plans for ballparks is New York's reconstruction of Yankee Stadium. It will leave us with a great sports landmark structurally mauled somewhat beyond need in our view.

But some Yankee Stadium is better than none, and that seemed to be the alternative choice.

The day of the individualistic ballpark is clearly passing. Candlestick Park, built in 1960, is now the second oldest ballpark in the National League. The great wave of concrete park construction began in 1909 and culminated with the original version of Yankee Stadium in 1923. It produced fourteen ballparks. Today, only four (not counting Yankee Stadium's revised structure) remain.

Ballparks hatch nostalgia in gushes. Baseball is a game of warm memories. It knows few experiences equal to an old Brooklyn diehard recalling days at Ebbets Field with its angular walls and jutting screens, an ancient Phillie follower reflecting on Grover Cleveland Alexander setting shutout records in tiny Baker Bowl, or a North Side Chicagoan describing frantic efforts to locate a ball buried in the Wrigley Field ivy as runners churned the bases. They don't make 'em like that anymore.

The ballpark is one aspect of baseball's history and character that has been dealt with, for the most part, in only isolated and incidental ways. This book is intended to bring the element of the ballpark and its relationship to the game into focus. Along the way, it may also capture for some the lost days of venerable old parks. It is nostalgia, perhaps more than any other element, that distinguishes baseball from its contemporaries among popular team games. The isolation of the individual player makes him more distinct and recollectible. The languid process of the game as well as the idiosyncrasies of the ballparks of a bygone era allows individual elements to stand out more vividly.

While the heart of any real fan who grew up with them will probably remain with the old, generally demolished ballparks of the age before franchise shifts, expansion, night World Series games, and synthetic surfaces, the new ballparks are not without their virtues. Broadly speaking, they incorporate much higher degrees of personal accommodation within their design, often bordering on the luxurious.

To provide an intelligible background for understanding the significance of the ballpark, some historical detail about the game is included. But it should be kept in mind throughout that this book is not a history of baseball. It is, rather, a history of baseball parks. Many stories are therefore included that have minimal impact on the broad scope of baseball history. But they illustrate some human aspect of ballparks and are presented for that purpose.

While this is in many respects a serious history, I have sought to avoid burdening the reader with a narrative cluttered excessively by scores and dates. The appendixes contain much reference information in tabular form that the statistically oriented reader may find a source of fascination.

At some points in the text, and in several of the statistical appendixes that accompany it, are facts that may not correspond to data on the same subject published by the club involved. As a matter of scholarship (and our own curiosity), we have tried to resolve through independent research any question or conflict.

Once case in point concerns the American League. Baseball historians almost universally ignore the maiden 1900 season. In our view this is fatuous. The American League began play in 1900 under its present name and with much the same leadership that built it into the familiar structure of today. It was a semiautonomous minor league. Most writers claim that it willingly accepted minor status and therefore was "not recognized" as a major league. The suspicion is that Ban Johnson never willingly accepted minor status, but rather saw it as a political ploy to enable him to build up his organization before challenging the old, established NL in full-scale battle. The historical argument is that the quality of play did not qualify it for major status even if such had been accorded by the rival National League. The quality of play was quite possibly comparable to that of the NL of 1876, the Federal League, the Union Association and Players League that have been accorded general recognition. At any event, the quality of play and the strategy that led Johnson to accept minor status for 1900 are not at issue in this book. The fact remains that the AL played games that year in eight cities, including Detroit, Cleveland, Chicago, Milwaukee, Kansas City, and Minneapolis, all now members of the league. Therefore, the tables for first games and other data, where applicable, indicate 1900 dates.

While other similar matters are discussed throughout the text, it should be most emphatically stated that this book would not have been possible without the almost-universal cooperation of the major league clubs' public relations directors and numerous other official baseball men.

The structure of this book is a bit unusual. After the initial chapter, the text is organized alphabetically by major league cities. Thus the entire story of all ballparks in, say, Boston, is found within its chapter. A franchise that shifted will have its history split among the cities in which it has operated.

Since the story of ballparks cannot be separated from the teams that play in them, a table is included among the appendixes showing the location of all current major league clubs throughout their history. Four National League clubs (the Dodgers, Pirates, Cardinals, and Reds) also played in more than one league, all tracing their origins to the American Association (1882–1891).

While coming generations may never know the glee of trying to guess at the crack of the bat whether a ball will carry against the Green Monster at Fenway Park, it is our sincere hope that this book will preserve a passing era, evoke some nostalgia, provide some information, and give as many hours of pleasure to those who read it as it has to those who prepared it.

BILL SHANNON

Acknowledgments

A project of this size and scope could never have been completed without much generous assistance. The authors are indebted to the public relations directors of those major league teams who responded to our many requests for aid. Particular appreciation is also due to Harry M. Stevens, Inc., the concessionaire, and two of Mr. Shannon's personal friends, Dave Hynes and Gerry Beatty, for permission to select freely from their unpublished collections of photographs. An additional credit goes to Mr. Hynes for his unselfish aid in researching myriad statistical details contained in the appendixes. Another sincere expression of gratitude is due Cliff Kachline of the Baseball Hall of Fame and National Baseball Library who also fielded a flood of inquiries without an error. Research was immeasurably aided by the kindness of Bob Wirz, public relations director in the Office of the Commissioner of Baseball, his American League counterpart Bob Fishel, and their respective staffs who were most patient with incessant requests for assistance. Likewise, the respective staffs of the New York Public Library and the Library of the Racquet and Tennis Club were most cooperative. Special note must be made of the efforts of John Smith, who kindly read the manuscript, and Joan B. Nagy, who edited it. Between them they not only managed to make this work readable but also flushed out many of the author's errors. For their responsiveness to many of the photographic needs of this book, thanks go to Jack Fletcher and his staff at UPI. Above all, the authors are grateful beyond words to Seymour Siwoff of the Elias Sports Bureau for his personal contribution to the research and for permitting the authors the run of his files for the statistical sections. To all of these, as well as Bill Gillenwater, Jay Chesler, Dick Schaap of *Sport Magazine*, Hayden Trubit, Elmo Celentani, Michael Burns, and other baseball buffs too numerous to mention, thank you.

The BALLPARKS

From Open Field to Superstadium

Baseball wasn't invented by Abner Doubleday in 1839 at Cooperstown, New York. It wasn't really invented by anybody anywhere. The game is the end product of thousands upon thousands of years of bat-and-ball playing by countless unknown humans.

The game was a popular recreational pastime in the early 1800s. Newly independent America sought to fulfill its need for outdoor exercise and entertainment. It organized numerous variants of baseball into contests between neighboring towns which often lasted an entire day or, in some cases, days. Eventually these occasional games became more frequent and regular clubs grew up which gave members an incentive to train themselves between games as well as enjoying the camaraderie of their fellows.

One such club was the Knickerbockers of New York. In 1845 one of its members, Alexander Cartwright, laid out a new set of rules to improve the game. He gave the club its permanent place in baseball history at the same time. Cartwright made the bases ninety feet equidistant, eliminated the right to put out a batter or runner by "soaking" or hitting him with the ball, and added several other sophistications which gave the game essentially the look it bears to this day.

The earliest organized baseball clubs, beginning with the pioneer Knickerbockers of Alexander Cartwright, were conceived as sports clubs for the recreation of the amateur gentleman. This is, in fact, how they functioned. But the dogged determination to retain those ideals led them to extinction in the face of baseball's ultimate development into professionalism.

By the early 1850s New York and Brooklyn, in particular, and most other cities along the eastern seaboard, had at least one organized ballclub. Baseball was quickly becoming a fad. Games between rival teams began to attract attention, and weekly newspapers were founded to cover and give publicity to their activities. A national organization of players was started and soon began conducting a championship series. In 1858 a three-game set between the teams of New York and Brooklyn was held.

The story of the ballpark began in a world that none today could recognize or even visualize easily. It was a world of strange sounds. Sounds of clattering horses' hooves hitting cobblestone as they had done for centuries past in the service of man. Sounds of the bales of hemp hitting the wooden dock. Sounds of iron fire gongs rallying the volunteers to their tasks on New York's congested streets. Sounds of gunfire at Fort Sumter and Fort Moultrie. Sounds of hissing gas lights and sounds of angry abolitionists. William G. Brownlow was a parson with a passion for the Union cause. In 1862 he published a book that attacked the stance of the Confederacy and further inflamed the emotions of an excited nation already at war with itself. In March the *Monitor* and the *Merrimack* launched the era of armored sea warfare in the waters of Virginia's Hampton Roads.

New York at the start of the year 1862 was strangely remote from "Mr. Lincoln's war." Of course, there were the strident voices of the local politicians (pro- and antiwar) and newspapers (also pro- and antiwar). But life went on apace. A milliner, Alexander T. Stewart,

3

opened a drygoods store on Broadway at 10th Street in the midst of the City's "Ladies' Mile"; it became A. T. Stewart and Co. and, later, John Wanamaker's famous department store.

A new era was also opening for baseball. Having been codified into its recognizable state by Cartwright, the "New York" style of the game became the national standard. With all clubs now playing essentially the same rules, intersectional rivalries developed. Top teams, like Brooklyn's Excelsior club of 1860, toured the country. But gentlemen's rules still prevailed.

Unlike baseball itself, the ballpark had an inventor. He was William Cammeyer, and in 1862 Cammeyer changed baseball forever. That year he introduced the first enclosed field for baseball playing. The Union Grounds, formerly the site of a skating club at Lee Avenue and Rutledge Street in the city of Brooklyn, opened on May 15.

Cammeyer was really expanding an idea that had been vaguely conceptualized a few years earlier. The very first "ballpark" wasn't a ballpark at all, but a race-track. The games of that 1858 championship series were played at New York's Fashion Race Course. About 1,500 paying fans anted up half a buck apiece to watch the first game ever played for a national baseball title. Ironically, the location of Fashion Race Course, that first ballpark, was but a few hundred yards from the present home plate at Shea Stadium. But it remained for Cammeyer to turn the fleeting idea into practical reality.

From 1845 until the 1860s baseball concerned itself primarily with the spread of the game's popularity and the uniform concept of the rules. The idea of professionalism had begun before the war through a desire to improve the local team by the addition of better players from outside the normal area of the club's territory. Each team also had the motivation, therefore, to reward its best players to keep them from moving on, as it were, to greener fields. This was essentially a minor breach in the amateur code that still ruled the game, though it was to have great consequences in the future. In 1866 the sub rosa professional player burst into the forefront of baseball attention. The national champions that year, the Philadelphia Athletics, were charged with paying three of their stars. It is highly likely that they were paying several others as well. The final chapter of the case was that a category of professional player was established by the ruling convention.

Since at least some of the players were now being paid openly, somebody had to undertake to see that this activity was administered in an orderly way. Thus, in its most infant form, the "front office" was born. Now, in addition to a playing captain who served the function of a manager, most clubs also had a president who served as business manager. Logically, the next step came in the actual ownership of clubs. But this development was still in baseball's future. Cammeyer was to accelerate its arrival.

The major motivating factor in this whole scheme now being money, the ballpark—which generated the revenue—began to assume paramount importance. Owners of enclosed ballparks, which appeared in almost every major American city after the Civil War, sought to increase their influence over the clubs and players. When the first professional league was established—the National Association in 1871—it was no surprise that William Cammeyer was the president of the New York entry. It was through the medium of the ballpark that the entrepreneur owner-manager gained admission to baseball. He was quickly to control it.

The proliferation of enclosed ballparks, which became a rage in the 1860s, presented Cammeyer with his first rival. He was met with competition in Brooklyn with the opening of the Capitoline Grounds, one of the most famous early parks. Its presence cost him the city's most celebrated and powerful club, the Atlantics.

Cammeyer, in the meantime, had struck a bargain with the most influential man in Brooklyn's arch rival sister city, New York. William Marcy Tweed, historically renowned as "Boss" Tweed and the father of the infamous Tweed Ring, had an all-pervading influence on civic affairs in New York. Tweed served variously as a city alderman, United States congressman, and state senator, all the while maintaining suzerainty over Mayor A. Oakley Hall. In addition to presiding over the looting of the city treasury by Hall and his other henchmen, Tweed also had control of the Mutual Baseball Club. The Mutual club had been organized by firemen in a New York company of the same name.

Since the firemen were beholden to City Hall for patronage and favors, Tweed was easily able to gain sway over the affairs of the ballclub. He saw to it that their games were switched to Brooklyn and, surprise, Union Grounds. It was more than an accident that the Mutuals, though hardly considered among the top rank of the New York ballclubs at the time, were the city's sole entrant in the National Association. It was also something other than coincidence that the Mutuals, though representing New York, played their home games at Cammeyer's Union Grounds in Brooklyn. Brooklyn was then an independent city; it didn't merge into the rest of New York until 1898.

Tweed's exposure, collapse, and imprisonment came in 1871 after the Mutuals (and Cammeyer) were firmly implanted in the Association. Without Tweed's backing, Cammeyer was unable to prevent the Atlantics from joining the Association (for the ten-dollar entry fee) as a Brooklyn club the next season. This left the Association with rival New York and Brooklyn clubs, both of whom, amazingly, played in the city of Brooklyn. But the crafty Cammeyer was equal to the occasion and endorsed a move to have Bob Ferguson, the star playing captain of the Atlantics, elected president of the Association.

Cammeyer doubtless believed that Ferguson's involvement in the divisive internal politics of the loosely organized Association would distract him from the work of maintaining the competitive strength of the Atlantics. If he, indeed, believed this, he was quite right. The Atlantics steadily deteriorated along with the Association itself. By 1875 the Atlantics finished a dismal last in the thirteen-team Association and were finished as a power in New York area baseball. Ferguson was also a declining star. He was no longer president of the Association, was shunted out of his managing captaincy by the Atlantics, and wound up in Hartford. He ultimately became an American Association umpire a decade later.

Following the 1875 season, the Association itself was on the ropes, and William Hulbert of Chicago led a successful movement to organize a new circuit. Cammeyer, comfortable in the knowledge that he had not only the only team in the already vital New York market but also his own park to play in, moved into the National League, which Hulbert organized. Cammeyer was, in reality, a personal prototype for the National League. He was not a gentleman player, but rather an entrepreneur owner-manager. Hulbert's new National League saw baseball as a business to be run by businessmen, not athletes.

The National Association's full title was the National Association of Professional Base Ball Players. Completely to the contrary, the National League was an organization "of Professional Base Ball Clubs" which placed the club owners and executives in a position of influential force. The owners were to hire the players on contract and determine the course of club affairs through a cadre of managers who were also hired. This economic view was fully in keeping with the prevailing trends then at work in the United States. It was the day of Jay Gould, Jim Fisk, J. P. Morgan, Andrew Carnegie, and the young John D. Rockefeller. The cash flow generated by the ballpark and its inherent capability to control entrance by patrons and charge them admission made it all possible.

Ironically, Cammeyer had sown the seeds of his own destruction as a baseball magnate. He misread the strength and determination of Hulbert and his followers. Feeling that the expense of traveling for the final few series of the 1876 season was not fiscally justified and, in fact, was quite likely to produce a loss, Cammeyer refused to send the Mutuals to the West. When Hulbert replaced Hartford's Morgan Bulkeley as National League president in December, 1876, he expelled the Mutuals and Philadelphia, which had adopted a similar point of view. Cammeyer's protests were unavailing and he then passed from the baseball scene. New York didn't rejoin the National League until 1883.

Ballparks also assumed a hand-me-down aspect during the period after the organization of the National Association. Association clubs moved along into the National League in 1876, and functioning clubs continued to use whatever park was available and best suited their need at the moment. The American Association was organized in 1882 and became the first rival to the NL, lasting until 1891. During that ten-year span, two other leagues were formed which became "third league" rivals for one season each. The Union Association of 1884 was a success only in St. Louis, and the Players League of 1890 wasn't really a success anywhere. But both left their residue of ballparks which were often scooped up by the surviving NL and AA clubs that had just lately been their competitors.

Although the Players League collapsed after its maiden season, it dealt a crippling blow to the American Association. Once again alone in the baseball marketplace, the NL absorbed some AA territory and expanded to twelve teams in 1892. But many of the teams proved uneconomic, and after the 1899 season four were dropped (Louisville, Cleveland, Washington, and Baltimore). Ironically, the cutback of 1899 opened the door for still another rival—this one to endure. The American League was functioning as the Western

Hoboken's Elysian Fields, first used by the Knickerbockers for match games in 1845, retained its position as a site for important games well into the enclosure era. The drawing above shows one of the National Championship series games in 1866. The site is now dingy industrial property. (*Photo courtesy of Baseball Hall of Fame*)

League in 1899, a Midwest minor circuit with Detroit, Milwaukee, St. Paul, and Minneapolis as its main markets. During the years it withstood the American Association, Union Association, and Players League, the NL clubs that survived gleefully picked up the ballparks they wished to occupy in each territory. Now the embryo AL was to adopt the same tactic.

Ban Johnson's thoughts were on problems other than ballparks when he changed the name of his Western League to the American League in 1900 and got permission from a nervous Cub management to install a team in Chicago that season. He also shifted a team from Grand Rapids, Michigan, to Cleveland's just abandoned League Park. In 1901 his club took over the former homes of NL clubs in Baltimore when outright war was declared between the American and National leagues. A year later, the new league moved into

an old NL park in St. Louis. By 1903, when peace between the leagues finally came, the AL needed to build only four new parks (Boston, Washington, Chicago, and Philadelphia) to establish itself as the permanent partner of the National League. The largest single outlay for a new team, a ballpark, had been neatly bypassed in all other cities by using buildings that formerly housed minor league or defunct NL clubs. Even at the turn of the century, renovation cost appreciably less than construction.

It was the American League that led the way into the next phase of the ballpark's history. Ben Shibe and his manager-partner, Connie Mack, determined to build a concrete park in Philadelphia. On opening day, 1909, the first new ballpark conceived and constructed from the outset of concrete and structural steel opened. Forbes Field, the first such NL park, opened in mid-

6

Ballpark creator William Cammeyer, while the owner of the Union Grounds, sometimes used the power of his position vindictively. In 1876, when the Arlingtons refused to lend his injury-ridden Mutuals their pitcher and catcher for an NL game against Boston, he canceled their remaining games in his park. (*Photo courtesy of Baseball Hall of Fame*)

season that year. By the end of the 1910 season, Cleveland and the Chicago White Sox had new concrete stands.

A final effort to establish a rival major league came in 1914 and 1915. Another aggressive minor league, the United States League, came under the control of glib James Gilmore, who renamed it the Federal League and found backers for a war with the two existing circuits. Unfortunately for Gilmore and his partners, the Federals were faced with a completely different ballpark condition than had prevailed just fifteen years before when the AL came into the field. The Federals had to build expensive new ballparks of concrete, brick, and steel in almost every city during the two years of the FL's existence. One of these, now familiar as Wrigley Field in Chicago, remains. Although the FL was modestly successful in luring fading stars and some young

talent for its teams, it was unable to overcome the twin economic handicaps of bidding for players and building parks.

Baseball can hardly lay claim to being the first modern mass spectator sport. Even in America both horse racing and boxing, among others, have a better right to such an assertion. But from the economic point of view, baseball built the entire foundation of professional team sports. Coming at a time when American industry and the ingenuity that spawned it were just beginning to flex their muscles, baseball proved to be the ideal medium for testing and perfecting the techniques of sports merchandising.

It can be safely asserted that the successful introduction of the ballpark, and its universal adoption, changed the game from a sport to a business. From the end of

Sportswriter Ban Johnson became president of the minor Western League in the 1890s and began laying plans to turn it into the American League. His aggressive club owners led the way into the concrete and steel epoch, four of the first five concrete grandstands being built by AL clubs in 1909 and 1910. (*Photo courtesy of Baseball Hall of Fame*)

the Civil War onward, the enclosed ballpark swept the baseball world. It becomes fully understandable then why the Cincinnati Red Stockings became the first entirely professional team in 1869, a scant four years after Robert E. Lee offered General Grant his sword in surrender at Appomattox. The ballpark, of course, was not the sole reason for the emergence of professional baseball; but it played a major part in that emergence.

Concession concepts, scorecards, the sale of telegraphic rights (forerunners of radio and television packaging), vending of souvenirs, off-premises production of collectible items such as sales promotion tools (picture cards, for instance) and sports coverage by the press (often against the better judgment of the editors) were all developed around major league baseball. Virtually all of these developments took place between the end of the Civil War and the close of the nineteenth century. The elaborate structure of the baseball industry, now widely imitated by all professional (and most collegiate) team sports, was constructed entirely on the foundation of the ballpark and its ability to produce the primary source of revenue: ticket sales.

During its developmental period, owners of ballparks sought to use other sports as sources of additional income. National League owners once seriously considered forming a professional football league as a satellite to their baseball operation. What we now familiarly call warning tracks in ballparks were originally introduced for use by racing bicyclists during the bike craze of the 1890s. Some parks, notably in St. Louis, were even converted for use as racetracks.

The so-called enclosure movement was the rage of baseball after the Civil War. Virtually every city engaged in the construction of a spacious wooden enclosure for the local baseball teams. These early ballparks generally were constructed by a private investor who, in most cases, did not control a club. Instead, they sought to rent the grounds to local teams on a per-game basis. In return for the use of the baseball grounds, the club permitted the owners of the enclosure to charge a minimal fee for admission to the games.

It didn't take long for the clubs to catch the notion. Soon they began demanding a share of the gate receipts. The owners of the enclosed parks, like Cammeyer, argued that they had taken the investment risk and responsibility for the maintenance of the grounds and its security. When the clubs pressed for a share of the cash flow, their fans often accused them of violating their basic amateur code. Thus, a three-cornered argument

developed. The entrepreneurs who owned the parks sought to keep the cash. Many clubs actively lusted after the profits of the owners. And some clubs (and many fans) still stubbornly lavished their love on the amateur ideal of the gentlemen's era with its open fields and leisurely spectator gatherings.

In the amateur days, games were played in open fields, and those who cared to amuse themselves by viewing merely arranged their forces at convenient points around the edge of the playing area. Admission was never charged and seldom even considered. The overhead was minimal, and the players looked upon what costs there were as an investment in their own physical fitness and recreation. Even when the famous amateur clubs began to tour the country, many of them refused to accept any money. The tour of the National club from Washington, D.C., as far west as Chicago in 1867 cost the team members and officials over $3,000.

By 1867, however, the largesse of the amateur clubs was already on the brink of becoming a memory. Baseball had begun its transition from elite amateurism for the gentlemen participants to competitive professionalism for the paying spectator. Human nature was beginning to take its toll on the high idealism of the 1850s that motivated the gentlemen players. The urge to win games became more significant than the sportsmanship and gamesmanship of recreation. Winning teams drew large and enthusiastic audiences; they also engendered strong civic support. The means to capitalize on these elements had already been introduced by Cammeyer and was shortly to revolutionize the entire concept of baseball. It also altered its purpose in the American society.

The decade following the opening of the first ballpark in 1862 saw such rapid growth in the number of enclosed parks and professional players that a league founded in 1871 was composed entirely of professionals playing in enclosed parks. At the start of that year there were only eighty-four registered professional ballplayers. But the National Association was formed for the purpose of playing professional games and charging admission to watch those games.

Cincinnati came forth with the first entirely professional team in 1869. That year, a crowd of over 15,000 paid their way into Brooklyn's Capitoline Grounds to watch a game between the local Atlantics and the Philadelphia Athletics. It was clear then that this sport could be a big business.

The enclosed ballpark also brought the entrepreneur

into baseball. He set the sport on the path to organization as a mass-appeal entertainment and business. Although the ballpark created overhead that had to be met, it also created a way for entrance to the grounds to be controlled and hatched an environment in which things of value could be sold—choice seats, refreshments, programs, souvenirs. Today such concessions form a vital element in baseball's profit picture, accounting for 15 percent of an average club's revenue, often the difference between profit and loss.

Ultimately, it was the enclosed ballpark that changed the entire nature of the game from low-scoring, defense-dominated contests into free-swinging, offense-oriented games. As the game and the men who played it outgrew the confines of the older ballpark, the explosive drama of the homerun came to the fore. The lively ball and the shrinking ballpark made this change possible. The need to expand capacity on a fixed piece of property was responsible for reducing outfield acreage and putting the fence within reasonable reach of every hitter. Today, 138-pound shortstops hit more homeruns individually in a season than league leaders did before the turn of the century.

Historically, the ballpark developed through several epochs. First there was the open field of the amateur days. Then, beginning in 1862, there was the enclosed wooden ballpark followed by the concrete and steel era, starting in 1909. In 1960 the massive superstadium phase began with the opening of Candlestick Park in San Francisco.

During all of these developments, property valuations remained a prime factor in ballpark location and construction. In its earlier stages the ballpark was located on the outer edge of the urban center to allow for the use of cheap real estate. With the growth of baseball as a commercial venture, the park began to move closer to key public transportation and nearer the center of the urban area from which it drew its audience.

When the Union Grounds opened, some of the more sports-minded newspapers in New York and Brooklyn hailed the idea. They were also quite pleased because the new park was accessible from both of the principal districts of burgeoning Brooklyn by the Flushing, Division Avenue, and Greenpoint horse cars.

In many cases the city grew around the ballpark and created the "inner-city park" (Ebbets Field in Brooklyn and Connie Mack Stadium in Philadelphia are among the handiest examples). Then came a second trend—to move the ballpark away from the urban center and surround it with the enormous inexpensive space needed to park the private car. Now the trend seems once again to be reversing itself. The ballpark is moving back into the center of the city (Riverfront Stadium in Cincinnati and Three Rivers Stadium in Pittsburgh are examples of this trend).

Over the years, many ballparks have been built on land previously used for other sporting purposes both before their construction and after their destruction. The granddaddy of all ballclubs, the Knickerbockers, played their early games in a field at 26th Street near Madison Square in Manhattan—then considered uptown. Four decades later Stanford White was to use almost the same site for his magnificent second Madison Square Garden. The Knickerbockers themselves moved across the Hudson River to Elysian Fields in Hoboken, New Jersey.

Cammeyer reversed the process by building his Union Grounds on the site of the old Union Skating Club. In Chicago, Charles Comiskey's first park was on the site of a cricket grounds. The original Polo Grounds was just what one might think, a polo field. But over the years, the lure of baseball has been so strong that ballparks have sprung up in locales that were previously brickyards, slums, lumberyards, swamps, and plain old vacant lots. Charles Ebbets had to acquire over 1,200 parcels of land for Ebbets Field.

The parks generated their own traffic habits and frequently affected the composition of the neighborhoods around them. In later years, the blade cut the other way as well, the neighborhoods often affecting the usefulness and attractiveness of the ballparks.

Once the clubs forced the ballpark owners to capitulate and allow a share in the gate receipts, both partners underwent profound changes. At first, the only gain for the players was a reduction in each man's outlay for new equipment and uniforms. But the wheels, once set in forward motion, drove swiftly and inevitably toward professionalism. Better players began to demand larger proportional shares than their fellows. Park owners sought to increase their direct influence over the clubs and assume managerial control of their business functions. In time, both were to succeed.

The amateur era was as good as dead. The avalanche of dollars fit the tempo of the times and swept aside all in its path. Among the victims were the fabled Knickerbockers. By clinging vigorously to their amateur precepts, they became dinosaurs, admired but not emulated, and passed into obscurity by the 1880s.

In the days that produced the first wave of ballpark construction, the innovation was widely acclaimed. Cammeyer's baby was credited with providing superior, well-graded grounds for the baseball clubs, plus reducing the hazards of fans interfering with play. By its mere existence, the enclosure instilled a more formal aura on the game and improved crowd behavior. It gave the game substance.

Cammeyer's invention was to have more far-reaching effects than were immediately apparent. The one to become most rapidly recognized was, naturally, money. Though the Knickerbockers continued to resist the trend and persisted in playing at Elysian Fields, other less altruistic clubs clambered onto the bandwagon of mammon. Cammeyer, who had charged ten cents per head from the outset at Union Grounds, was less than enthusiastic about this. He resisted sharing the proceeds with all his vigor before finally yielding. But, he was eventually to solve the problem by becoming not only the owner of the ballpark, but the team that played there as well.

Despite the ignominy of his removal, William Cammeyer's legacy to baseball was enduring. All ideas seem obvious in retrospect, but Cammeyer's innovation of the ballpark as a fully enclosed field with a seating capacity was the most revolutionary thought in the game's growth since Cartwright standardized the bases at ninety feet. To his detriment, Cammeyer was unable to balance properly the value of public confidence in the integrity of the schedule against the short-range dollars-and-cents considerations. But even his departure from the National League served a valuable purpose. Owing to a squabble over his dismissal, the NL adopted a regular schedule for 1877 drawn out in advance by the league and enforced on the member clubs. This replaced the sloppy and informal home-and-home arrangement of the previous years which left scheduling of precise dates to the teams involved.

The second fundamental result of the Cammeyer ballpark was upon the game itself, although it was much slower to develop. As originally conceived, the ballpark was designed to keep out nonpaying cranks (as baseball fans were then known). Built entirely out of wood, all early ballparks had enormous outfield areas and the fences were great distances from the infield. As the ballparks and the games played within them changed, the fences became targets for hitters to drive balls against or over. Thus the simple matter of enclosing the park gave

rise to the most important strategic changes in the game as well.

Initially, the pioneer Union Grounds had a seating capacity most reliably estimated at about 1,500. This consisted of benches principally reserved for the ladies who might be in attendance. It also had a clubhouse for three teams and some primitive refreshment service. The remainder of the audience observed the former custom of standing around at various points on the edges of the playing field. It wasn't long, however, before additional seats and benches began to sprout up. Union Grounds had increased its capacity to about 6,000, including standees, before the first National Association season in 1871. On January 20 of that year, Ivers W. Adams led a group that resolved to invest $15,000 in a new corporation to bring a National Association franchise to Boston. They began by hiring Harry and George Wright from Cincinnati. Baseball, as a business, was on its way.

During the first twenty years of the enclosed ballpark, all of the structures were built of wood and were of relatively simplistic design. The sophistication of the baseball industry quite naturally led to the increased sophistication of the ballpark. Chicago was among the early leaders in elaboration of the basic ballpark. In 1885 the new West Side Park at Congress and Loomis streets opened to raves for its luxurious appointments, which included "a neatly furnished toilet-room with a private entrance . . . for the ladies." The main grandstand was horseshoe shaped with 2,500 numbered seats and its adjacent bleachers held 3,500 more. The entire layout was surrounded by a brick wall twelve feet high. For the well-to-do and civic dignitaries, a dozen rooftop boxes were provided with individual chairs.

The wooden ballparks, regardless of their development or lack thereof, were seldom the exclusive property of the big league club. As noted earlier, they were in many cases owned by somebody other than the club. Even in those situations where the National League team owned the park, it was frequently made available to other local teams. Until the NL abolished its rule against Sunday games in 1892, almost all League parks were used by semipro or amateur teams on Sundays and many other days during the week when the club was on the road. It was not uncommon for three or four games to be played in a big-league park on a Saturday when the professional team was engaged elsewhere. This activity had several direct results. One was that the route to the ballpark became a very familiar one in the community. Another was that constant use tended to lend a pasturelike quality to the playing field. Owners of ballparks, even when they were the clubs themselves, were not notorious before the turn of the century for lavishing care upon their fields. The number of groundsmen responsible for the field was kept as low as possible—sometimes even lower.

Wooden construction was, of course, not the only difference between the older ballpark familiar to today's generation and their wooden predecessors. The wooden parks were much smaller in capacity, rarely exceeding 15,000. The box seat at field level, which is so common today, was almost unknown. After the introduction of the boxes, they were placed in the forward portion of the stands; but the front row of the box seats was usually five or six feet above the level of the field. Thus, the dugouts were not dugouts at all, but often-uncovered benches placed in front of the stands. In some of the later wooden era ballparks, the dugouts were tucked under the front of the boxes, creating something of a "dug-out" effect. Most ballparks lacked dressing rooms for the visiting clubs (Chicago was an exception to this) and teams, dressed in full uniform, were generally taken to the ballpark in carriages. This practice led to a virtual street parade prior to every game, often accompanied by trumpets or even small bands and, depending upon the visiting team, a stray vulgarity or two from the sidewalk.

Another major difference came in the size of the outfield. The playing area of the average wooden park was huge by today's standards. The parks were not normally built with stands or bleachers in the outfields, although some were added in the 1890s. The fences were placed at the outermost edge of the lot occupied by the park. This was frequently 500 or more feet from the plate. In the era of dead-ball baseball, the homerun was not a major factor of strategy for several reasons, and the distance to the fences was certainly one of them.

The enormous outfield areas led to another common practice that tended to reduce the number of homeruns. On Saturdays and major holidays, the crowds that overflowed the tiny grandstands were herded into the outfield, where they filled in an area in front of the fence and behind rope or chain barriers set up for the occasion. Balls hit into the crowds were generally grounds-rule doubles or triples when, normally, some of them might have rolled far enough to be homers.

Wooden parks were constantly in a state of flux. Some teams changed parks regularly in the early years of professional baseball. Fire was a constant danger throughout the wooden era. One of the most critical fires in baseball history, from the club standpoint at least, probably occurred in Louisville. After having been a charter member of the NL, Louisville was a major league city as a member of the American Association from 1882 to 1891 and the NL after 1892. In midseason 1899, the main grandstand at the Colonels' Park was destroyed by fire. A temporary stand was hastily erected but failed to provide suitable capacity. After a doubleheader with Baltimore in August created havoc with overflowing fans, owner Barney Dreyfuss decided to shift his home games to other cities until something could be done about the park. The last NL game was played in Louisville on September 2, 1899. All remaining games were played in the home parks of the opposing clubs, and the Colonels were among the four clubs dropped by the NL at the end of the season, never to return. Dreyfuss became president of Pittsburgh and took, among others, Honus Wagner to the Pirates with him.

In the long run, Dreyfuss may have profited from the events in Louisville. With Wagner and the other Colonel stars, Pittsburgh became an NL powerhouse. But it was more than chance that brought Dreyfuss to build the first "fireproof" concrete park in the National League, Forbes Field, in 1909.

Probably the worst single season for fire was 1894, when NL parks in Baltimore, Philadelphia, Boston, and Chicago were either damaged or destroyed by fire. The new style concrete ballpark freed the owners of many difficulties attendant to the operation of a wooden facility, the most persistent being fire. The last of the wooden parks was Robison Field in St. Louis, which was used until 1920. But two of the last wooden parks, the Polo Grounds and Washington, burned in the spring of 1911. Both were replaced with concrete structures.

Initially, the concrete parks followed the mode of the wooden ones in that the outfield walls were great distances from the plate. But their very permanence gave rise to new needs, requiring expansion of the existing rather than constantly shifting from one park to another. When the earliest concrete parks were built, they had walls often 400 feet or more from home plate at the foul lines. To increase the capacity for the major attractions, ballclubs added extra stands in the outfield which had the simultaneous result of permanently reducing the homerun distances.

Parallel with the concrete park came a jump in costs to build parks to the new major league standard. By the time the Feds threw in the towel at the end of the 1915 season, every major league team except the Cardinals was ensconced in a new facility. The grand finale of that era—Yankee Stadium—didn't come until 1923 when the Yankees shifted to the Bronx after a decade as tenants of the Giants in the Polo Grounds.

Baseball's explosive growth after 1900, the popularity of the World Series, and the swelling of urban population in the big-league cities created both the need and the financial resources to build new parks. Once built, it became necessary to generate funds to maintain them, pay taxes on them, and staff them. During its period of consolidation, the NL saw its clubs gradually get control of their ballparks for the most part. During the entire concrete era, all ballparks were constructed by the clubs that used them. For mainly economic reasons, they made them available for pro football, college football, boxing, and other noncompetitive attractions, but seldom for baseball on any level. With the coming of the superstadiums, ballpark construction costs soared beyond the reach of most clubs. Since 1960, seventeen new ballparks have been built and only one was financed entirely with private capital. That solitary exception is Dodger Stadium in Los Angeles, which opened in 1962. All others have been erected with public money from city, county, state, federal, or some authority treasuries. Thus the major league clubs have gone full cycle. From tenant to landlord to tenant. Only three American League clubs still own their own parks, and they are the three oldest in the majors: Chicago (1910), Boston (1912), and Detroit (1912). In the NL only two privately owned parks remain: Wrigley Field (1914) and Dodger Stadium.

Gone are the colorful and magnificently archaic structures that once dotted the baseball landscape. Shibe Park (or Connie Mack Stadium), Forbes Field, Sportsman's Park, League Park, the Polo Grounds, Griffith Stadium, Crosley Field, Ebbets Field, and Braves Field have passed into history. Many of these venerated sites were anachronisms within a few years after their construction. Yet the individualistic ballpark,

an anachronism though it may be, breeds speculation and statistical oddities that serve as the perhaps unequaled sources of baseball conversation. This is the lifeblood of the "hot-stove league." Baseball needs this speculation as fuel for the million mini-wars of words that made it the paramount sporting game of America. When Mel Ott retired in 1947 he held the National League record for career homeruns with 511, but he never hit a homer in Philadelphia's Shibe Park. Ted Williams playing in Yankee Stadium would quite probably have broken Babe Ruth's record long before Henry Aaron; Mickey Mantle playing in Ebbets Field might have set a record no man could ever have approached. The loss of the old ballparks, in many ways, is baseball's loss. Ballparks hatch nostalgia in gushes, and baseball is a game of memories.

Another immutable fact is that ballpark operations, per se, are not profitable. This is why ballclubs have increasingly sought to get out from under the obligation of building and maintaining them. It is also why it is absurd to expect ballparks to pay off their bonds, let alone produce public profit. The economic value of the ballpark must be measured in other terms. Its great worth in civic unity, often neighborhood revitalization, and continuing national exposure via the press probably justify the millions in public funds poured into them in recent years. It is also likely that a touch less luxury here and there would have saved many of these millions. And greater variety in construction certainly would have been more than welcome.

Space-age gadgetry is now the byword in ballpark construction, with fountains, waterfalls, light shows, exploding scoreboards, escalators, posh clubs, and form-fitting chairs now the order of the day. The new parks have, at least in the short run, broadened the base of baseball attendance and brought women and families in record numbers. But we've been down this path before. The major attraction is still baseball, and the hard-core baseball fan is still the most important customer. The more things change, the more they seem to remain the same. A fan can see fountains in a city park, light shows on a tote board, and go to a posh club anytime he has the money. But the only place he can see baseball is at the ballpark. The only thing the ballpark can give him that he cannot get anywhere else is baseball.

Anaheim

From a ballpark point of view, the California (née Los Angeles) Angels certainly got around when they were younger. The American League expansion of 1961 gave birth to a Los Angeles franchise that played its first season in Wrigley Field, its second through fifth at Chavez Ravine, and its sixth at Anaheim Stadium. Apparently the Angels like custom housing, since Anaheim Stadium was built with them in mind and there they have stayed.

When the Angels were created, their owners sought permission from Los Angeles officials to play their American League home games in the Coliseum, which was then serving as a temporary home for the Dodgers while construction was underway in Chavez Ravine. Walter O'Malley was somewhat less than receptive and pointed out that he held an exclusivity clause for baseball in the Coliseum as part of his contract there. But the Dodger president also suggested that if the Angels were willing to play in Wrigley Field, it would be available. Built in 1930 for the Pacific Coast League Los Angeles Angels, Wrigley Field was a pretty little park which also had a pretty little capacity. The Dodgers had acquired it in a package deal from the Chicago Cubs during the 1950s as a preparatory step toward moving from Brooklyn.

The Cubs held the PCL franchise in Los Angeles and therefore had the territorial rights to the area for major league baseball under the league rules at the time. The Dodgers sold the Cubs their Fort Worth, Texas, team for the Los Angeles PCL club and got Wrigley Field as part of the package. The Angels agreed to play there and also, subsequently, to become tenants of the Dodgers when the new Dodger Stadium opened the following spring.

In 1961 the little ballpark on 42nd Place had a seating capacity of 20,543 which had been tested more than once by the old PCL club. There was some concern about the new American League being bottled up in the teenie Wrigley, but it was never a serious problem since the new Angels never drew a crowd of over 20,000 for any game that season.

The thing they ran up big numbers for was homeruns. General manager Fred Haney, the former Pirate and Brave manager, realized he had a minor league park on his hands and big-league opposition on his schedule. He also knew that it took time to build the key element of victory, pitching. So he went for the next best thing, power hitting.

Wrigley Field's comfortable confines were tailor-made for long-ball shows. It was 339 feet to the right corner, 340 to left, and a reasonable 412 to center. But to the glee of hitters and the terror of pitchers, Wrigley Field hung in at a snug 345 feet in each power alley, where the real consistent long-ball damage is done.

Anaheim Stadium was the site of the 38th All-Star Game in 1967. Starting at twilight for an eastern television audience, the game turned into the longest marathon in All-Star history. The Nationals finally won, 2–1, in fifteen innings. Despite heavy usage by high school, junior college, and college football teams each year, Anaheim Stadium retains both its integrity as a baseball park and its excellent natural grass playing surface. (*Photo here and on next page courtesy of California Angels*)

Haney thus grabbed off such heavyweights as Leon Wagner, Steve Bilko, and Ted Kluszewski to trade big blows with the visiting sluggers. Wrigley Field led the league that season as the homer-hitters paradise. But the Angels finished eighth.

The Yankees drew the year's largest house (19,930) for a night game on August 22, but the final major league crowd of 9,868 on October 1 was more typical of the season. In fact, the entire final series with the Cleveland Indians was typical of the Angels high-scoring, one-year hiatus at Wrigley Field. On Friday night, September 29, the L.A. sluggers won 6–4. The next night they bombered the Indians again, 11–6, and Cleveland general manager Gabe Paul was so annoyed he fired manager Jimmy Dykes after the game.

Coach Mel Harder handled Cleveland on Sunday, and he must have known something. The Tribe won the third slugfest, 8–5, as four homers were hit. One was a grand slam for Cleveland by Walter Bond. Wagner and Bilko both connected for the losing Angels. Mudcat Grant was the last major-league winning pitcher at Wrigley Field and, curiously, former Yankee relief star Ryne Duren took the loss (his thirteenth of the season).

In 1962 the Angels moved into Dodger Stadium; but they didn't call it Dodger Stadium. Then publicity director Irv Kaze went to great lengths to get everybody to refer to it as Chavez Ravine (at least when the Angels were home). But no matter what you called the park, it did something for the Angels. In May a fun-loving eccentric named Bo Belinsky pitched a no-hitter, by June the Angels were real pennant contenders, and by season's end American League attendance in Los Angeles had virtually doubled over 1961.

Bill Rigney guided the Halos home in third place that year and might have done even better if the Yankees weren't still the scourge of the American League, winning their third pennant in a five-year skein that didn't end until 1964.

Still, the Angels third-place finish was the highest ever recorded by an expansion team in its second season. During a series with the Yankees that July, L.A. pulled the largest crowd in the history of the franchise into Chavez (53,591) and finished the year with 1,144,063 paid customers.

But during the succeeding seasons at the Dodgers' home, the Angels kept losing ground. From third, they tumbled all the way to ninth in 1963, and by 1965 attendance had skidded to 566,727, lowest in the Angel annals. That season was also the last one in Chavez Ravine. On September 2 team president Gene Autry announced that the club was changing its name to the California Angels prior to moving into the new stadium being assembled for their tenancy at Anaheim, some miles south of Los Angeles.

George Brunet hurled a shutout as the Angels beat the Red Sox, 2–0, in their final game at Chavez on September 22, giving L.A. a record of forty-six wins and thirty-four losses in their last year there. When they left, the Angels took with them many pleasant memories as well as one dubious distinction. On September 19, 1963, a makeup day game with Baltimore drew 476 fans, the smallest crowd in Dodger Stadium history. On that day the Dodgers were glad to call it Chavez Ravine.

Anaheim Stadium

Popularly known as the Big A around the southern California area where the fans follow their baseball on portable radios, car radios, and big beach radios, Anaheim Stadium is an Orange County neighbor of Disneyland. It is also one of the nicest facilities in major league baseball for viewing as well as playing a game.

Anaheim Stadium is unique in its construction. Although used for literally dozens of high school, junior college, and other football games every year, it was designed as a baseball park—and that is what it is. The Big A has avoided all the pitfalls of oval and circular parks. It is built along the classic lines of the baseball park with straight sides following the foul lines and bending gently around behind the plate.

Aside from the pitching of Nolan Ryan, the dominant feature of Anaheim Stadium is the giant scoreboard in left-center field. Shaped like an enormous A, the board is encircled near its top by a halo forming the Angel symbol. The two legs of the board spread further apart as they move toward the ground, and suspended between them is an electronic flashboard that relays information on the game, other results, news notes, and plugs of various kinds.

The three-tier stands are virtually all in foul territory, there being no seats in the outfield. Though the listed capacity is 43,204, the record attendance for a game is 44,631 against Oakland in 1971, and capacity has been exceeded on a couple of other occasions as well.

Built by the Del Webb construction firm, Anaheim Stadium was opened on April 19, 1966, when the White Sox beat the Angels 3–1. But the opening day loss didn't deter the fans from welcoming their new club with a record 1,400,321 attendance for the season.

In harmony with its completely suburban environment, Anaheim Stadium is surrounded by parking spaces for 12,000 cars and seeks constantly to generate interest in ways to get to the park. With the increasing concern of citizens over the use of automobiles, the Angels promote bus connections from all of the motels in the stadium area. On a normal night, a half-dozen buses run routes that are advertised by the club to collect fans who don't wish to drive. For those who do, the club advises patrons about the best routes. In 1974 a new superhighway (the Orange Freeway) was largely completed, which club officials were hopeful would relieve some traffic on State College Boulevard, one of the main routes to the park.

Southern California is almost entirely dependent upon the car for transit. But the Angels encourage fans to come, among other methods, by bicycle. One of the major bikeways in the area crossed nearby Orangewood Avenue and the Angels have built extensive bike racks near a main gate to the park adjacent to the VIP parking area.

One of the more unusual incidents in Anaheim Stadium history occurred on the final night of the 1970 season. On that night Alex Johnson, the much-traveled outfielder, was lifted from the game by manager Lefty Phillips when his batting average reached .329, enabling him to win the American League batting title by .0002. Phillips and Johnson later became the central figures in a clubhouse feud which led to both of their departures from Anaheim.

Atlanta

If no other game had ever been played there, Atlanta Stadium earned its niche in baseball lore on April 8, 1974. That night, before an overflow crowd of 53,775 and a national television audience, Hank Aaron socked a homerun into the Braves' bullpen in left field off Al Downing of the Dodgers. That homer, of course, was Aaron's 715th career circuit and enabled him to surpass the career total of Babe Ruth. Coming on a raw, damp night, the Aaron homer sent the greater part of the packed house streaming toward the exits. Most of them never came back.

Atlanta, with its long and colorful tradition with the Atlanta Crackers of the Southern Association, welcomed the Braves with open arms when they were transplanted from Milwaukee in 1966. During the first six seasons in Atlanta Stadium the Braves drew season attendance totals in excess of one million. In the first season it was a record 1,539,801. Then, when the figures were starting to drift downward, the Braves won their division title in 1969 and attendance jumped back up.

Since then the trend has been steadily downward. But one thing that has not declined during those years is the homerun production in Atlanta Stadium. During the four seasons prior to Aaron's record-setting blast, the Braves' ballpark had been the leading homerun target in the major leagues. In 1970 the Braves combined with the visiting hitters for 211 homers in the Atlanta park. The figure for 1971 was 186, for 1972 it was 174, and in 1973 back up to 205. The Braves' batters alone accounted for 118 homers in Atlanta Stadium in 1973.

That year three Braves (Hank Aaron, Dave Johnson, and Darrell Evans) matched or exceeded the forty-homer mark for the season.

Apparently to slow things down a bit, the Braves added 10 feet to the right center power alley in 1974, stretching it from 375 feet to 385, although all of the other dimensions in the park remained constant. Interestingly, with the departure of Aaron prior to the 1975 season, the Braves elected to add ten feet to the power alley in left center, increasing it to 385 feet also.

The climatic conditions in Atlanta and the structure of the ballpark seem to combine to help hitters get the extra loft to boost the ball over the six-foot high fences that surround the outfield.

One of the elements that helps the hitters in Atlanta is the enclosed nature of the double-decked stands. The partial roofing of the upper deck runs completely around the circle of the stadium's shape, cutting down some winds that might blow across or into the path of a batted ball. The enormous number of homers (visiting Cincinnati had sixteen alone in 1973) led the Braves' pitching staff to nickname the park The Launching Pad.

Another reason for the inordinately high homer totals in Atlanta is that it is radically different from most other parks in the National League's West Division. It has, for instance, a natural grass surface. It is a good park for a sinker-ball pitcher. A pitcher can throw high and hard at Dodger Stadium and get by because the ball doesn't carry as well. He can throw a sinker at Cincinnati and get buried by hard grounders shooting through the fast artificial infield. But in Atlanta a good sinker is

Located a mile south of downtown, Atlanta Stadium is within sight of the Georgia State capitol building. The maze of superhighways between downtown and the stadium provide quick access for fans from throughout the southeast, who are a large part of the support for the Braves. (*Photo courtesy of Atlanta Braves*)

One of the first circular ballparks, Atlanta Stadium was completed in 1965 by Thompson & Street Company. In 1971 the All-Star Game was played under the lights and the NL won, 4–3, in ten innings. (*Photo courtesy of Atlanta Braves*)

Atlanta Stadium was the site of the first division-playoff game in NL history. This was the scene on October 4, 1969, when, despite a homer by Henry Aaron, the Braves were beaten, 9–5; by the New York Mets, who won the NL pennant two days later. Chief Noc-A-Homa is in the left-field corner behind the fence. (*Photo courtesy of Atlanta Braves*)

the pitcher's best friend. Breaking-ball pitchers like Phil Niekro and the matured Carl Morton have done well there, often throwing shutouts. A power pitcher who tires in the late innings can have real problems here.

As those who viewed Aaron's homer became aware, the bullpens in Atlanta are located behind the wire inner fence. Behind them is the outer wall, which extends up to the lower deck of seats. The outer wall is adorned with advertising which gives the park both a local flavor and a colorful vintage look that contrasts with its architectural composition. Behind the wire fence in almost dead center the Braves in recent seasons have kept Levi Walker, Jr., a full-blooded Indian, costumed as a brave with the fanciful name of Chief Noc-A-Homa. Noc-A-Homa comes out of his teepee and does a war dance when a Brave hits a homerun or on other similar special occasions. Dancing for homers in Atlanta has been almost a full-time job in recent seasons, but Walker also serves as a goodwill ambassador for the club and makes personal appearances.

The dominant feature of the stadium's exterior are large riblike verticles that extend from ground level upward to the top of the park, curving with the outer contour of the building onto the roof. Unlike many other new superstadiums of its type, Atlanta has its light units mounted on the roof's front facing and they, too, are a prominent feature.

Atlanta Stadium is located slightly under a mile from midtown Atlanta at the junction of three major interstate highways and is easily seen from the Georgia State Capitol. In fact, it is bounded on the first base side by Capitol Avenue.

Baltimore

Baltimore has a long baseball tradition but it is, to say the least, an uneven one. Lord Baltimore was among the strongest of the principal independent clubs during the days before the formation of the National Association, and when the Association began in 1871, it was among the charter members.

Several other clubs from the city on the banks of Chesapeake Bay were prominent during the early years of professional baseball. But it was in 1882, when Baltimore joined the embyro American Association, that the city really came of baseball age. Baltimore's first substantial ballpark was built by the owner of the AA club, Harry Von Der Horst. It was Union Park on 25th Street (then known as Huntingdon Avenue) near Greenmount Avenue. It had a large double-decked grandstand with small bleachers attached and held 6,000, large for a wooden park of the time.

By the 1890s Union Park was expanded to hold 9,500 seats, but it frequently contained crowds of double that size during the championship years of the Orioles in the NL. It had additional attractions as well, since an amusement park was adjacent. The park provided dining, dancing, and band concerts for twenty-five cents after the baseball games.

Union Park cost $5,000 to build and included chairs in the main grandstand behind the catcher as well as the twin bleachers, which held 2,500 fans each. The entire park was enclosed by 40,000 feet of wood fencing. The additional capacity was accommodated, in the custom of the day, by standing room.

When the AA disbanded in 1891, the Orioles were among the surviving clubs invited into the NL. Managed by Ned Hanlon, the Orioles were then to embark upon their greatest era. Hanlon was eventually to be responsible for the return of baseball to Baltimore, but only after his involvement in Brooklyn cost the city its NL club. His new Orioles in the International League set the stage for Jack Dunn and the preservation of the Oriole tradition on a minor league level when the American League abandoned the new Oriole Park in 1902.

Hanlon's major contribution to Baltimore baseball history, however, was the creation of the club that made the Orioles the scourge of the NL during the 1890s. A team of tough, scrappy, and scientific players, the Orioles counted among their stars John McGraw, Wee Willie Keeler, Wilbert Robinson (later manager at Brooklyn), and pitcher Bill Hoffer, who recorded a record of seventy-eight wins and twenty-four defeats during one three-year stretch in the 1890s. The Orioles won the NL pennant in 1894, 1895, and 1896, and were contenders most other years during the decade.

But 1894 brought Baltimore not only its first pennant, but also a disastrous fire (of somewhat suspicious origin) that nearly destroyed Oriole Park. If fire was the major danger to the wooden ballpark, wood was also a material compatible with quick reconstruction, and by season's end the Orioles had a ballpark complete with flagpole from which to fly their newly won pennant.

But even more than fire, it was front office machinations that really damaged the Orioles. Following the death of Brooklyn owner Charles Byrne, Hanlon and Brooklyn club secretary Charles Ebbets formed a plan.

Hanlon remained as president of Baltimore, but became field manager at Brooklyn. Many Oriole stars were transferred to the Dodgers by Hanlon and helped Brooklyn win the 1899 NL pennant. Both Hanlon and Ebbets felt more money could be made with a winner in Brooklyn than in Baltimore.

As a result of this unsavory arrangement, Baltimore was one of the clubs dropped when the National League determined to reduce twelve clubs to eight at the end of the 1899 season. The former NL club was succeeded by a new entry called the Orioles in the upstart American League in 1901.

AL president Ban Johnson thought the opening in Baltimore so significant at the time that he personally threw out the first ball on April 26, 1901, passing up an opening in Philadelphia on the same day. A crowd of 10,371 showed up for a pitching matchup between the famous Iron Man Joe McGinnity and Bill Kellum of Boston. Neither pitcher was very impressive, but Balti-

more rewarded the crowd with a 10–6 victory sealed by four runs in the eighth.

Within less than two seasons, however, the picture of joy turned dismal in Baltimore. McGraw, a notorious umpire baiter, was engaged to manage the new Orioles; but he had a bitter battle with Johnson, who sought to maintain strict control of the game in the hands of the umpires, and jumped the club in 1902 to take the New York Giants' job. The team's on-field performance was less than sensational, and the attendance was reflective of the won-lost record. Johnson decided that Baltimore was the club he was going to shift to New York in his continuing war with the National League. When word of this leaked out, audiences in Oriole Park virtually vanished. On September 29, 1902, Boston beat the Orioles, 9–5. It was the last AL game played in Baltimore by that club, which was shifted to New York over the winter to become the Yankees.

Jack Dunn became something of a baseball legend by

After the old Oriole Park burned down in 1944, Baltimore built Memorial Stadium. The Triple-A Orioles played in a football field before moving to the original version of the stadium in 1949. The original stands, demolished in 1954, were in what is now center field. (*Photo courtesy of Baltimore Orioles*)

serving as the discoverer of Babe Ruth. But his signing of the orphan from St. Mary's Industrial Home was certainly not Dunn's only claim to baseball fame. He was also the guiding light of the International League franchise which functioned as Baltimore's professional baseball team for decades.

But Dunn was to face an almost fatal challenge in Baltimore in 1914 when the Federal League war broke out. Ned Hanlon, the former Oriole, returned to the city as the head of the syndicate that owned the club in the outlaw league. To make matters even worse, Hanlon built a large wooden ballpark for his club directly across the street from Oriole Park. The new Terrapin Park was ultimately to start a chain of events that was finally resolved in the United States Supreme Court.

Dunn, aware of the strength of the Terrapins' challenge, asked the Giants and McGraw to play an exhibition against the Orioles on the day of the FL opening across the street. Unfortunately for Dunn, the Terrapins were a much better draw than he imagined. The always popular Giants drew a scant crowd (generously called 1,000) on April 13, 1914. Meanwhile, across the road, some 23,000 fans packed into the new park to watch Mayor Preston throw out the first ball and the Terrapins squeezed past Buffalo, 3–2, in the first FL game ever played.

The competition of the Terrapins drove the Orioles out of Baltimore by 1915, and when the FL folded at the end of that season the Terrapins were not consulted by the other seven Federal League owners concerning the peace terms. Baltimore was the only FL club that even approached showing a profit. The other owners were simply weary of the conflict, but Baltimore brought a suit against organized baseball that finally found itself on the docket of the Supreme Court in 1922. The Terrapins lost the suit with Justice Oliver Wendell Holmes making his famous decision finding that baseball was not governed by the ordinary rules of trust and monopoly.

Memorial Stadium

The Dunn family continued to operate their International League club in the 14,000-seat Oriole Park after the settlement of the FL war. After the old park burned down in 1944, the triple-A club played in a football field. In 1949 a new 30,000-seat Memorial Stadium was built and the Orioles moved in for what proved to be a brief stay. On October 29, 1953, came an announcement that beleaguered Bill Veeck had sold his St. Louis Browns to a Baltimore group that was shifting the AL team to Memorial Stadium. But even the new AL Orioles retained a link with the old days by having Jack Dunn III serve as a director of the club.

It was Dunn's IL team that was displaced by the major league move that was to bring about a virtual reconstruction of Memorial Stadium. Built and operated by the city and county of Baltimore, the park was rebuilt so that the stands in what is now center field were demolished and a new grandstand was erected that is still being used. A second deck was built atop the single-tiered stands, expanding the capacity by 50 percent. Major concession and accommodation installations were made to handle the anticipated larger crowds for major league baseball.

The anticipation was an accurate one. On April 15, 1954, Baltimore returned to the big leagues and a crowd of 46,354 showed up to celebrate the occasion. Young Bob Turley pitched a seven-hitter and struck out nine Chicago White Sox, Clint Courtney and Vern Stephens hit homers, and the celebration was complete. Baltimore won 3–1. Despite the early triumph, the new Orioles were really the feeble old Browns dressed up in different uniforms. They performed with a style that betrayed their incompetence and finished the season with only 54 wins in 154 games. But the continued stumbling on the field was tolerated and the early enthusiasm was enough to produce a creditable attendance in the million-range.

Meanwhile, Paul Richards of the White Sox was hired as the principal baseball man in the organization. It was Richards who engineered one of the largest trades on record. For trivia buffs, the deal began on November 18, 1954, and wasn't completed until December 3. The Orioles acquired nine players from the Yankees in exchange for eight. From New York came outfielder Gene Woodling; pitchers Harry Byrd, Bill Miller, and Jim McDonald; catchers Hal Smith and Gus Triandos; and three infielders, Willie Miranda, Don Leppert, and Kal Segrist. Baltimore gave up pitchers Bob Turley, Don Larsen, and Mike Blyzka; catcher Darrell Johnson; outfielders Jim Fridley and Ted del Guerico; and infielders Billy Hunter and Dick Kryhoski. This, at least, gave a new look to the Orioles.

But when the packed crowds did show up for an occa-

Memorial Stadium originally held 31,000. The stadium was entirely rebuilt and double-decked for the new Orioles, who were the moribund St. Louis Browns, purchased by the Baltimore group from Bill Veeck. In recent years, the park has become the center of local controversy over its supposed inadequacies. (*Photo courtesy of Baltimore Orioles*)

An aerial view during the 1966 World Series shows overflowing Memorial Stadium. A new scoreboard has been installed recently and the center-field area is now filled with hedges and other landscaping, reducing the capacity slightly but improving the ambience considerably. (*Photo courtesy of Baltimore Orioles*)

sional big game, it was sometimes difficult to see what was going on. In the 1953 reconstruction, Memorial Stadium had been blessed with the most unusual support poles in the major leagues. The upper deck is supported by enormous fat cement columns that screen off vision in all directions for rows behind. The Orioles now seldom sell these seats and when they do, they are sold on an obscured vision basis.

Memorial Stadium was perhaps even more unique in its time for not having a roof over the upper deck. It was the first ballpark to be constructed with an open-air topside. When first opened, Memorial Stadium had hedges running around the center-field portion of the outfield. In 1954 Mickey Mantle lost a homerun to Jim Diering of the Orioles on a sensational catch in the hedges.

Shortly thereafter, a 7-foot high wire fence was installed in the outfield from right center to left center, reducing the distance to 410 feet in straightaway center. In addition, the capacity was slowly increased. During the off-season between the 1960 and 1961 seasons, 2,571 new box seats were installed, which raised the capacity to 49,375. Further additions in recent years have increased it to 52,137 (excluding the rarely sold 864 seats buried behind poles).

During the more than two decades of its major league existence, the field dimensions have changed little. Memorial Stadium has a shape similar to a pair of crescents which converge behind home plate. This semioval configuration has given the stadium tight corners. It is only 309 feet to the left- and right-field foul poles but breaks away sharply to 385 feet in left and right center. The center-field distance has remained at 410 feet since the installation of the wire fence. The spacious power alleys permit good pitching by fast ballers. Few homers are hit down the lines, though they sometimes come at inopportune times.

During the 1957 season, the White Sox had a game "won," 4–3, in the ninth. The game was due to be halted by a prior-agreement curfew at 10:20. Paul LaPalme of Chicago would face, at most, one batter in the home ninth. He threw, as it turned out, one pitch. That was hit out of the park for a homer which tied the game. Baltimore won the replayed tie later in the season. The batter was Dick Williams, later pennant-winning manager at Boston and Oakland. A disconsolate Bob Elson told his Chicago radio audience, "I would have thrown that ball on the screen." Unfortunately for LaPalme, his pitcher's instincts made him throw a strike.

Ballparks tend to reflect the city in which they are located. This is certainly true of Memorial Stadium. Underneath its stands is a veritable bazaar of local goodies. Chief among them are the submarine sandwiches and seafood specialties that are local favorites.

In recent seasons, many fans have had the opportunity to enjoy these edibles during the World Series. After a near-miss in 1961, the Orioles slumped into noncontention for a few more seasons. But 1966 saw a pennant fly over the city of Baltimore for the first time since 1896. The Orioles repeated their championships in 1969, 1970, and 1971 and won eastern division titles in 1973 and 1974.

The Orioles won the World Series twice in four tries. But the 1966 triumph was one of the most astonishing of all time. The Los Angeles Dodgers had won the National League pennant with a team built around the powerhouse pitching combination of Sandy Koufax and Don Drysdale. Now any schoolboy knows that pitching wins a short series, and the Series is a short series. The Dodgers were prohibitive favorites. But they lost to the Orioles in four straight, igniting delirium in Baltimore.

But for all the brilliance of Brooks Robinson, Jim Palmer, Boog Powell, and Frank Robinson, for all of the glory of the championship years, Memorial Stadium has become the center of civic controversy. In the mid-1970s a struggle developed between the Oriole ownership and local officials over the need for a new stadium. The Orioles suggested they might leave the Baltimore area if one wasn't built in the near future. If this does come to pass, they might surround it with 40,000 feet of wooden fence and call it Oriole Park—just for old times' sake.

Boston

The history of baseball in Boston goes back almost to the game's organized beginnings. The proper Bostonians played their own version of the game many years after the rest of the country switched to the New York Game of Alexander Cartwright. But once they abandoned their "Massachusetts Game," which was played in a rectangular rather than diamond form, they made up ground in a hurry.

When the National Association was organized in 1871, the Boston club was one of the charter members. The Athletics of Philadelphia won the first NA pennant, but Harry Wright's Boston powerhouse won the final four before the Association broke up after the 1875 season.

From that point on, Boston was established as a hotbed of baseball and until 1952 was one of only two franchises continuously active in the National League from its first season of 1876. Nathaniel Appolonio was president of the club during its first NL season, but the club then fell under the control of Arthur Soden. Once quoted as saying "Common sense tells me that baseball is played primarily to make a profit," Soden ruled the Boston club's affairs with an iron hand from 1877 to 1906.

During almost all of those thirty seasons, the team that became the Braves played in the South End Grounds. This property on Tremont Avenue was the site of a field that was rebuilt and altered a half dozen times over the years of Soden's reign. Once he even tore out the press box to increase the seating capacity.

Boston won NL pennants in 1877, 1878, and 1883 before slipping into an eclipse that lasted into the 1890s. The somewhat unexpected pennant of 1883 not only increased attendance during the latter part of the year but inspired Soden to expand South End Grounds in anticipation of even larger crowds in 1884. Interestingly, the pennant-winning teams of 1877 and 1878 had shown losses of $2,230.85 and $1,433.31 respectively. But Soden hoped increased enthusiasm would turn the tide in the 1880s. In many respects it did, but Soden's own frugality may have had even more to do with the positive change in the club's financial condition. Under the leadership of Frank Selee, the Braves finally re-emerged as a power, but not before surviving their first real challenge for the Boston market. In 1890 the Players League established a very popular club in the city which won the PL flag. When the circuit disbanded, much of the team shifted into the American Association and again won a pennant. But when the AA also folded up, the Reds did likewise and left the field to the Braves.

Pitcher Charles Nichols was the star of the Braves' championship clubs in the 1890s, winning 297 games and losing only 147 from 1890 to 1899. He won 30 or more games for a record seven straight seasons as Boston won pennants in 1891, 1892, 1893, 1897, and 1898. In the midst of this renaissance, Bobby Lowe became baseball's first four-homer hitter in a single game when he turned the trick on May 30 at the old Congress Street Grounds.

A disruptive event on May 15, 1894, explains how Lowe came to be playing at Congress Street in the first place. The Braves and Baltimore were engaged in the second of a three-game series with the Orioles having taken the opener. With Boston coming to bat in the third, a commotion broke out in the right-field bleachers. This little triangular piece of the wooden park was new, having been installed to replace the old center-field bleachers, which were ripped out after the previous season. The fans in the higher-priced grandstand beneath its twin spires hooted at the crowd in the twenty-five-cent seats and called "play ball" to the players. But it shortly became evident that the right-field seats were on fire. Within a matter of minutes they were completely ablaze and most of the crowd of 3,500 began running for exits. Those gathered in left field at the furthest point from the fire were gradually menaced as the fire spread along the wooden fence. They made good their escape through a hole in the center-field fence.

Once outside, the fans saw an astonishing sight. The South End Grounds, one of the most elaborate and famous ballparks in the country, was being completely swallowed up by flames. The tall spires collapsed with a rush of seared timber and fire-scorched air. As the fire companies began to arrive, the entire area was encased in a haze of smoke. The fire leaped across Tremont Street and began spreading through the residential neighborhood. Before it had ended late that night, the blaze had consumed 164 wooden buildings, destroyed 13 brick buildings, caused damage estimated at between $500,000 and $1,000,000, and left a thousand families homeless. By some grace, no deaths were caused.

Soden switched the Braves' games to the old Congress Street Grounds, which had formerly housed some of his competitors. South End Grounds, valued at more than $75,000, was insured for only $40,000. When it was rebuilt, the once magnificent park was scaled to the size of the insurance check and became one of the most notoriously small and cramped of all major league parks.

But uncomfortable though it was, the Braves evidently enjoyed the new surroundings. Not only did they regain their pennant-winning form but, in 1897, ripped off a seventeen-game winning streak. Of the seventeen, all but one game was won in South End Grounds.

In 1901 another challenger came into Boston. The Boston Red Sox of the American League rivaled the Braves for the territory that, a half century later, they were to win. The Red Sox built a new home on Huntington Avenue where Northeastern University now has its indoor athletic building. The new wooden park had a capacity for 7,000 plus a few thousand extra in the outfield. The Huntington Avenue Grounds became dis-

tinguished because the first four games in the history of the World Series were played there in 1903 against Pittsburgh. But it was clear the Red Sox had no future there. On June 24, 1911, club president John I. Taylor announced that a new park of concrete was to be built in the fashionable Back Bay area.

Although Soden had died, his influence lingered. The Braves continued to struggle in South End Grounds. Then, suddenly, they burst forth with a late-season surge that is now one of baseball's great sagas. Coming from last place on the Fourth of July, traditional midpoint of the baseball season, the Braves won the 1914 NL pennant. However, the Series games with Philadelphia were played in the Red Sox's new Fenway Park for its larger capacity. In 1915 the Braves unveiled their plans for a new home on the sight of the Allston Golf Club on Commonwealth Avenue. The wooden ballpark era in Boston had finally ended.

Fenway Park

Fenway Park remains today as the most alive of the world's living museums. Colorful and misshapen, Fenway is also neat and beautiful. A nightmare to left-handed pitchers, it is a dream for fans. Recalling the bygone days with a visual power beyond description, Fenway Park is truly a baseball landmark. Its giant wall snugly enclosing the left-field into an area of seeming Little League proportions brings drama and suspense to every game. The single-deck stands bring a warmth and intimacy to baseball now unknown in any other environment.

Of course, when Fenway Park was opened it wasn't intended to be a museum, landmark, or anything but a ballpark. Its uniqueness and longevity have made it special to baseball, but it remains very much a ballpark more than anything else.

The Fenway Park of today has changed little in forty years. When Thomas Yawkey bought the Red Sox in 1933, Fenway Park was still largely wood except for the main grandstand. The following year he had it entirely rebuilt and gave it the present appearance.

It was opening day for the rebuilt Fenway Park, and Boston's fabled mayor James Curley was among those on hand to see the historic park's 1934 rededication. (*Scorecard from Shannon Collection*)

The Commonwealth Avenue trolley provided a convenient trip to Braves Field, but some folks wanted to show off their Maxwells, Fords, Grahams, and Pierce-Arrows anyhow. The result was this scene when the park opened on August 18, 1915. The turf in Braves Field was replanted from the old South End Grounds. (*Photo courtesy of UPI*)

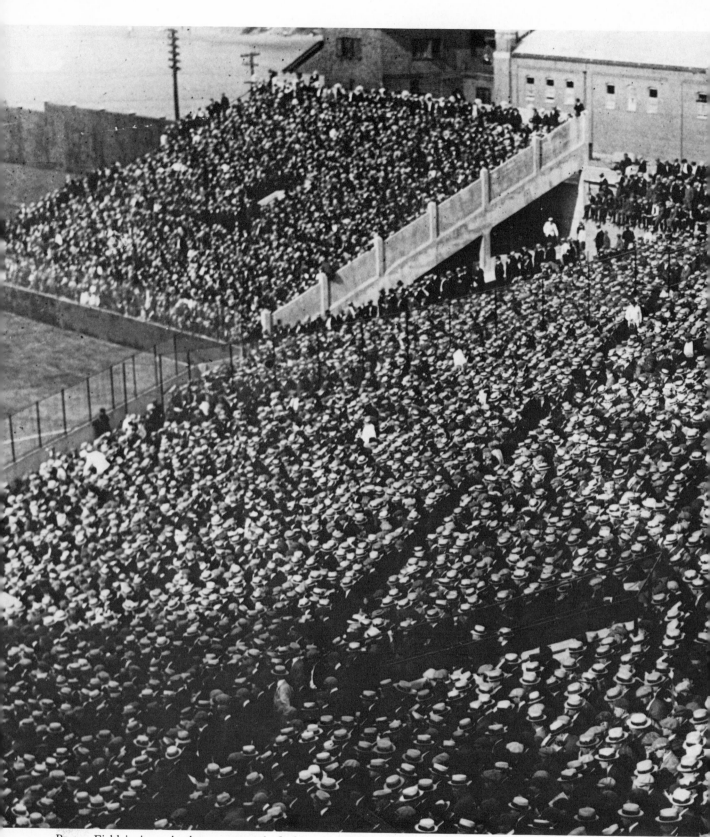

Braves Field in its early days saw crowds flocking to ticket windows on Gaffney Street, fans packing the right-field pavilion and famed "jury box" bleacher, and the remnant of the "Miracle Braves" of 1914. Fans here saw a twenty-six-inning game, the longest in the big leagues, in 1920 against Brooklyn. Both pitchers, Leon Cadore of the Dodgers and Joe Oeschger of the Braves, pitched complete games in the 1–1 tie. (*Photo here and photos on next page courtesy of UPI*)

Fenway Park's reconstruction was handled with care by the Osborn Engineering Company of Cleveland, the most active and experienced hands in ballpark construction during the great concrete and steel era. Wooden bleachers in right field were ripped down, as was the wooden wall in left field which had been covered with enormous signs advertising a wide range of products, local and national, over the years. Also removed was "Duffy's Hill," the incline patroled with distinction by famous Sox outfielder Duffy Lewis. But when the reconstruction itself began, Fenway Park was restored to its unusual proportion and retained its distinctive character. Yawkey eventually did away with the advertising signs except for the small board above the roof in the right-field corner that carries the message of the Jimmy Fund, which might be described as the Red Sox's "house charity."

The exterior of the brick grandstand on Jersey Street was virtually untouched, and the original keystone bearing the words "Fenway Park 1912" remains above the ticket windows leading into the box seats behind home plate. The tree-lined Jersey Street side of the ballpark captures most appropriately the atmosphere for a day at Fenway. Replace the cars with carriages and the scene could be much like it was on opening day six decades ago when the Red Sox outlasted the Yankees, 7–6, in eleven innings.

Fenway saw its first World Series games at the end of its very first season of use. The Red Sox won their first AL pennant since 1904 and upset the New York Giants of John McGraw in the Series. Series games were also played at Fenway in 1914, although the Red Sox didn't win the pennant. The Braves, still based in South End Grounds, rallied to win their "miracle" pennant and used Fenway for the post-season classic games against Philadelphia. The Red Sox did win pennants in 1915, 1916, and 1918 but then went into a prolonged drought which saw them go without a flag until 1946. Since then only the sensational 1967 team has been able to bring a pennant to Fenway.

The Fenway Park that served as home for the American League portion of the 1946 and 1967 Series was somewhat different than the earlier one. In the reconstruction of 1934, the right-field dimensions were altered, and subsequent minor changes also affected right field. When originally opened, Fenway was only 313 feet 6 inches to the corner in right. In the 1920s it was moved back to 358 feet when a new bleacher was built

on the lot behind the park. In 1934, the new concrete stands in right field were only 302 to the corner but then curved away sharply to 380 in the power alley.

Easily the most familiar feature of Fenway is the Green Monster—the huge wall in left. It has always been a part of the park. Originally, it was 320 feet 6 inches down the line. Due to some shifting of home plate, it is now 315 feet, though there are pitchers who swear it is 115. For sheer height, the Monster is a baseball record-holder. It is 37 feet from base to top. To cut down on window breakage in the stores on Lansdowne Street, a 23-foot netting was placed atop the wall some years ago. Balls hit into the netting are homers. After a game, one of the Fenway attendants does a catlike walk along the top of the Monster to collect balls hit into the net during the game.

The netting got a major workout during one of baseball's most dramatic series in 1949. Joe DiMaggio, the heart and soul of the Yankees, had been sidelined for the first sixty-five games due to surgery for spurs in his right heel. A crowd of 36,228 turned out to watch his return in a crucial Fenway meeting on June 28. DiMaggio's single and a walk to John Lindell set the table for a three-run homer by Hank Bauer in the early going that helped the Yankees to a 5–4 win which ended a four-game Boston winning streak. The next afternoon the Sox built up a 7–1 lead after four innings. DiMaggio homered off Ellis Kinder with two on in the fifth. The Yankees tied the game in the seventh, when Gene Woodling doubled with the bases loaded. Then DiMaggio smashed an Earl Johnson pitch that cleared both the wall and the screen in left for the decisive run in the eighth. On Thursday, a paid house of 25,237 was swelled by a Ladies' Day audience and the crowd watched as DiMaggio socked a towering three-run homer off the light tower in left center with George Stirnweiss and Tommy Henrich on base for the deciding runs in a 6–3 Yankee win.

The Yankees went on to win the pennant on the final day of the season for their rookie manager, Casey Stengel.

Heartbreaking as the loss to the Yankees in 1949 was, the end of the previous season was even more grievous for Sox fans. The only regular season to end in a tie in AL history was decided at Fenway after the Sox tied Cleveland for the 1948 pennant. The powerful Red Sox lineup of Ted Williams, Vern Stephens, and Bobby Doerr was able to collect only five hits off the Indians'

Gene Bearden. Cleveland raked starter Denny Galehouse and reliever Ellis Kinder for thirteen hits and won, 8–3, to win the flag under the single-game playoff system then in vogue in the American League.

Despite the disappointments, Fenway Park has seen brilliance by such Sox stars as Ted Williams, Dom DiMaggio, Jimmy Foxx, Doc Cramer, Carl Yastrzemski, Bobby Doerr, Mel Parnell, Smokey Joe Wood, the young Babe Ruth, and many others. But, perhaps more significant, Boston fans have been treated to an endless succession of madcap finishes and thrilling games ranging from sublime to outrageous in Fenway.

Braves Field

Braves Field, at opening the largest park yet built, was one of the last of the concrete and steel stadiums constructed in the early years of this century. It was also used for less time than any of its contemporaries.

Francis Ouimet, the fabled golfer, once trod the ground on which Braves Field was built—it having previously been the Allston Golf Club, site of several major golf tournaments before World War I. But in 1914 the Braves acquired the site for their new home and set about building a massive structure. A much less ornate park than many others of the era, Braves Field was broken up into four major components. The main grandstand which ran behind home plate to just past the bases at first and third, large bleacher-type sections extending from the end of the grandstand into the right- and left-field corners, and a little bleacher in right—popularly known as the "jury box"—comprised the seating sections during most of the park's years.

One of the unique features of Braves Field was its access by trolley cars on the Commonwealth Avenue lines. The cars were able to turn off of Commonwealth into the ballpark and thus deliver the fans almost at the gates. On the Gaffney Street side of Braves Field was a large stucco building that served as the team's business office and also contained ticket arcades through which fans could pass directly to seats in the right-field pa-

vilion or the main grandstand. These windows did sensational business on August 18, 1915, when the park opened with a crowd of over 40,000—the greatest in the history of baseball at that time.

What they saw was a ballpark with an almost cavernous appearance. Down the line in left field was a distance of 402 feet, stretching out to 520 feet in dead center, and a healthy 365 down the right-field line. In the era of the less than lively ball, these distances were formidable.

They also saw a Brave team, which defeated St. Louis 3–1 that day, continue its pursuit of the Phillies for a second straight NL pennant. The Braves, however, were to finish second, seven games to the rear of Philadelphia. When the World Series was played, it was still played at Braves Field. The Red Sox won the AL pennant and, exchanging the favor of the previous season, moved their games into the new park.

After 1915 the Braves began steadily to decline as if the ghost of Arthur Soden had wished them ill. Following the move from ancient South End Grounds where they won nine NL championships in thirty-nine seasons, they were to capture only one in thirty-seven years at Braves Field.

The attendance at the huge new edifice declined in concert with the team's fortunes on the field. Bottom was hit during the war-shortened 1918 season, when only 84,938 fans found their way through the turnstiles to see a seventh-place team. After Emil Fuchs became president of the Braves, he sought to help out the attendance by adding seats—not because the extra seats were needed, but because he could put them in the form of a bleacher in left field and cut down the enormous distance to the wall. Homeruns fell into the new stands like hail but most of them were hit by the visiting team. Thus, halfway through the 1928 season, the new stands were removed after an experiment of less than one season.

The outfield dimensions at Braves Field were to undergo a series of almost annual rearrangements during the remaining history of the park. In the mid-1930s, it was 376 feet to right, 407 to straightaway center, and 368 to the wooden fence-within-a-fence in left. The inner fence in left was moved in and out several times without affecting seating capacity until, finally, in 1946, Braves Field was reconstructed for the last time. The field was turned slightly to shorten the dimensions and part of the stands down the first base line were cut out

The Huntington Avenue Grounds was the home of the Red Sox in the early AL days and the site of the first World Series game ever on October 1, 1903. Above is a typical scene from turn-of-the-century baseball—fans strung out across the outfield. Note the full-size broom to the left of the plate for the umpire's housekeeping duties. (*Photos left and above courtesy of Baseball Hall of Fame*)

The peculiar belly of the right-field wall and the towering Green Monster in left are but two of Fenway Park's distinguishing features. Despite talk of obsolescence, Fenway attendance topped AL clubs five times in eight years, from 1967 to 1974, and ranked second the other three years to Detroit's Tiger Stadium. The tiny capacity is a stimulant to advance sales and exciting games produce a heavy repeat business. (*Photo left courtesy of Dave Hynes; photo right courtesy of Boston Red Sox*)

in the right-field corner to permit the shift. The capacity was then reduced to 37,746.

The measurements of the playing field during the final years of Braves Field showed 319 feet to right, 390 in deep right center, 370 to center, and 337 down the line in left. Young Eddie Mathews took full advantage of the new shape of the park in his rookie year of 1952 to bang out twenty-five homeruns. The wall in front of the "jury box" stands in right was 10 feet high while the wall in left was 25 feet in height, giving Braves Field some of the feeling of Fenway Park, a few stops down the trolley tracks in Kenmore Square.

But the attendance and the team performance never really approached the level of consistency produced by the Red Sox; and this, ultimately, was to spell the doom of Braves Field. The team drew a million fans for the first time in 1947, hit a Boston NL record of 1,455,439 in 1948, and steadily drifted downward to 281,278 in 1952. The changing economics of baseball made the figure in 1952 almost ludicrous.

In March 1953 owner Lou Perini suddenly announced that the Braves would shift to Milwaukee for the coming season, and television news shows across the country showed film of the 1953 Boston tickets being dumped out of windows in the Braves office into a truck on Gaffney Street. But the announcement wasn't really a surprise. The decline of attendance almost to the point of disappearance had spelled the end of the Braves in Boston long before the formal announcement was made.

The farewell shot was fired in 1948, when the Braves

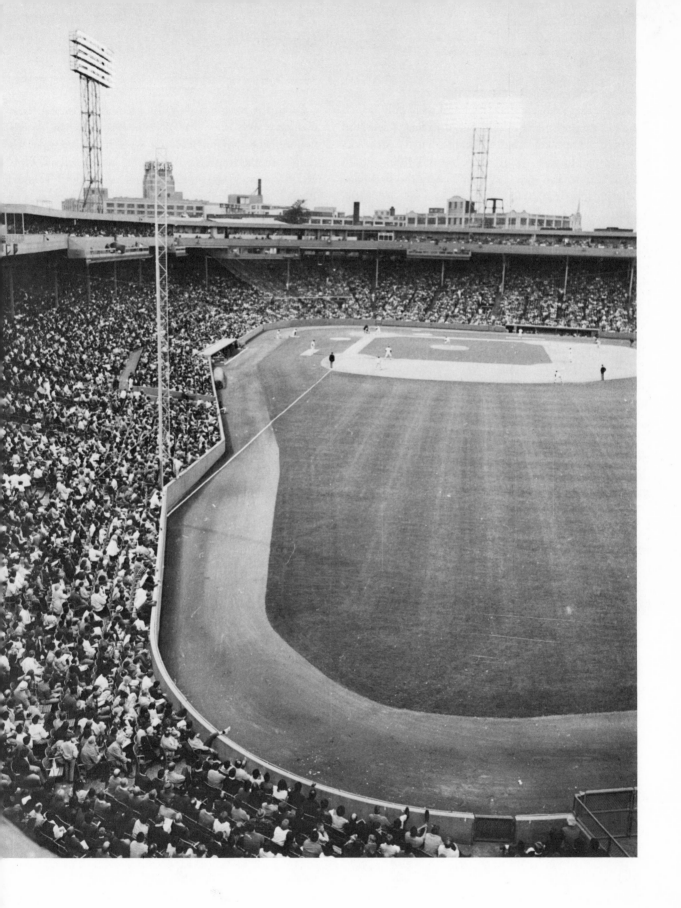

won their first pennant since 1914 and their only one in the concrete park. The World Series against Cleveland produced some memorable highlights, but it was a victory for the Indians. Warren Spahn and Johnny Sain ("Spahn, Sain, and Pray for Rain") were the backbone of the pitching staff, and third baseman Bob Elliot the big hitter for the 1948 Braves.

The final games played at Braves Field involved the Brooklyn Dodgers, who clinched a tie for the 1952 NL pennant with their victory in the finale. Brooklyn swept the last three games, winning a 1–0 thriller over Spahn on Saturday. On Sunday, September 21, the Dodgers fell behind, 2–1, in the fourth on two unearned Boston runs. But they routed Braves starter Jim Wilson with a six-run eighth and won 8–2. In the following day's editions of *The New York Times*, Roscoe McGowan commented that 8,822 fans showed up for the final Braves' home game "and many of them seemed to be Dodger fans." He was probably right.

The Braves Field of the Three Troubadors (fans who roamed through the stands during the 1948 pennant drive), Wally Berger, Shanty Hogan, Rabbit Maranville, and George Stallings was finished.

Behind it were left only the memories. Among those memories was the 1936 All-Star game, when an announcement that all reserved seats had been sold left fans with the impression the game was a sellout. Only 25,556 plus 15,000 empty seats saw the National League score its first victory of the series, 4–3. The crowd was the smallest in All-Star history. Other memories include the first night game played in Boston on May 11, 1946; the game in which Hall of Famer Paul Waner got his 3,000th hit; the first Boston Sunday baseball game; and the longest game by innings (26) in baseball history. That came on May 1, 1920, when Leon Cadore of Brooklyn and Joe Oeschger of the Braves went the distance in a 1–1 tie finally halted by darkness. Then there was Sunday, September 31, 1951, when a homer by Bobby Thomson helped the New York Giants beat the Braves, 3–2, on the final day of the season. The win enabled the Giants to tie the Dodgers for the NL pennant. All of this remains as the legacy of Braves Field.

Brooklyn

Brooklyn. Though out of organized baseball for nearly two decades, the very mention of it in a baseball context conjures up swarms of memories from the serious historian of the game to the youngster just becoming initiated to it.

The first Brooklyn ballclubs were organized in 1852, just seven years after the famous Knickerbockers formalized the game. Ten seasons later it was to serve as the birthplace for the enclosed ballpark when Union Grounds opened on May 15, 1862.

After the Mutuals were thrown out of the National League in 1876, it was Charlie Byrne, doubtless more than any other man, who was responsible for the development of Brooklyn as a fertile territory for professional baseball. Initially, Byrne operated a club in the minor-status Interstate League. He then obtained a franchise in the American Association in 1884, moved the team out of the tottering Association in 1889, and took it into the National League, where it became a fixture for almost seven decades.

Byrne was feeding an already well-fueled appetite. Brooklyn had been a hotbed of baseball since the 1850s, when clubs like Excelsior and the Atlantics were ranked among the nation's finest teams. The 1860 Excelsior club starred young Jim Creighton, the finest pitcher of his day. Union Grounds, by virtue of its position as the first of the enclosed fields, was a top choice for major games even when they didn't involve a New York or Brooklyn team. The Brooklyn cranks vigorously supported their clubs and the game with an enthusiasm that is still legend. The raucous fans of Ebbets

Field were but an end product of this unbridled enthusiasm.

Almost every war between rival leagues in baseball's early history had Brooklyn as the battleground for one of its vital skirmishes. At various times, the American Association (twice), the National League, and the Federal League operated Brooklyn clubs. Once, in 1890, the season began with three major league clubs in the city.

One of baseball's most famous early games took place at Capitoline Grounds, principal rival to the Union Grounds as the chief enclosed park of Brooklyn. On June 14, 1870, the Atlantics defeated the celebrated Cincinnati Red Stockings 8–7 in eleven innings. The victory sent hundreds heading to Mike Henry's (a popular bar and hotel) and ended Cincinnati's unbeaten streak, which had encompassed the entire 1869 season and all of 1870 up to that day. The Atlantics were the finest team produced by Brooklyn during the amateur era and won the National championship 1864, 1865, and 1870. Another Brooklyn club, the Eckfords, had won it in 1862 and 1863. In all, Brooklyn clubs won the National title six times between 1858 and 1870.

By the late 1860s baseball was a major item on the Brooklyn activity schedule, and in 1869 some 15,000 fans jammed into Capitoline Grounds to watch the Atlantics and the Athletics, then the defending National titlists. Thereafter crowds of that size became commonplace. By now all of the major clubs had moved from their open lots into the major enclosed parks. Previously, the Excelsiors had played at Smith, Hoyt, Car-

Mary Ebbets, daughter of the Dodger owner, tugged a bit but was able to hoist the flag on opening day in the brand new Ebbets Field. Within three years the 1916 World Series was played there and yet another pennant went up the pole in 1920; but there were no others until the 1941 club started the great Dodger championship streak. (*Photo courtesy of UPI*)

In the second of its three incarnations, Washington Park looked this way. Overflowing with 23,876 fans on July 6, 1907, the sight of the packed wooden stands gladdened Charlie Ebbets's heart. To the right can be seen horseless carriages on the field.

roll, and President Streets and then moved to Smith, Sackett, Hoyt, and DeGraw. The Atlantics began in Bedford before going to an open field at the Fulton Ferry House. The Eckfords played at the Manor House field in Greenpoint before going to Union Grounds in 1862. The Baltics initially played at 81st Street and Second Avenue, and the Putnams in Williamsburg.

Once the National Association was organized, the Mutuals became one of the big Brooklyn attractions even though they were technically a New York club. One of the first "crucial series" in professional baseball history was played at Union Grounds in 1871. Chicago came into town leading the NA standings by a half a game over the Mutuals. On June 5, 6,000 fans stuffed themselves into Union Grounds for the game between the two teams. Another 3,000 surrounded the park to watch the game from the tops of houses, carriages, and wagons. The Mutuals won 8–5 and went into first place. But they eventually faltered, and the pennant came down to the final game between Chicago and the Athletics of Philadelphia. Since Chicago's grounds were burned in the Chicago fire, the game was played at Union Grounds on October 30. Philadelphia won 4–1 and took the first NA pennant.

The next year the Atlantics joined the Association and played in the Capitoline Grounds. But they had

already begun to fade. The Mutuals were not serious contenders after 1871. Boston won the next four pennants and then the NA shut up shop, the Atlantics sinking with it. The Mutuals got expelled from the new National League after its first season and Brooklyn was without a club in the only significant professional league.

Henry Chadwick, the country's premier authority on the game, and the four Brooklyn newspapers were still considered powerful. But now they had to travel to cover all the major games since Brooklyn didn't have its own club in the late 1870s or early 1880s. It was Charlie Byrne who was to change this situation. On May 12, 1883, his Interstate club played Trenton in the first game ever played at the new Washington Park.

That opening minor league game drew 6,000 fans and the 23rd Regiment Band to play for the opening ceremonies. Brooklyn won 13–6. The continued support of the fans convinced Byrne that he should try for bigger things. After the season he applied for an American Association franchise. The AA magnates, not ignorant of Byrne's Brooklyn attendance, issued him one. On May 5, 1884, the AA came to Brooklyn when Washington was beaten 11–3 as Brooklyn unleashed a fourteen-hit attack and profited from ten errors.

From that point, Washington Park became the focal point of Brooklyn baseball. In the late 1880s the St.

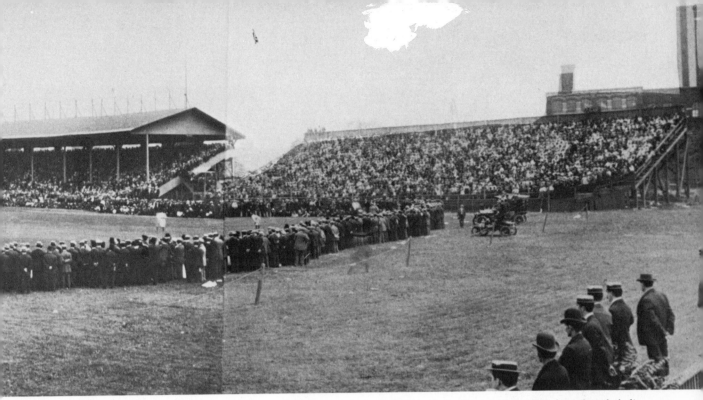

Elmer Stricklett pitched the Dodgers to a 7–0 win over Chicago and that gladdened the hearts of the full-skirted and dedicated ladies standing in center. (*Photo courtesy of Baseball Hall of Fame*)

r of Buffalo slashes out the first FL hit of the season at Washington Park in 1915. The Brookfeds added batting champ
.auff to their roster that season, but by the close of the campaign attendance had dwindled and the FL folded. (*Photo
of UPI*)

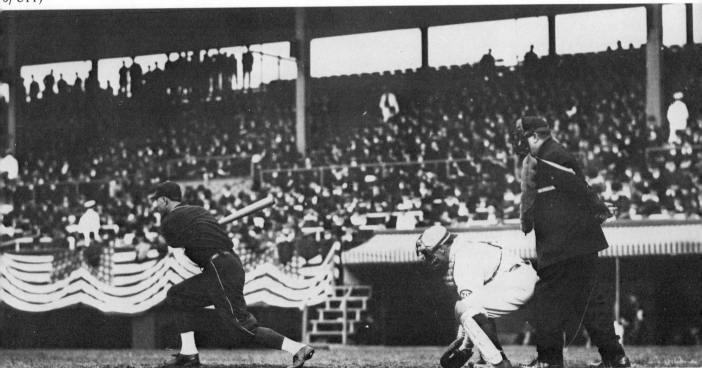

The reconstructed Washington Park in Brooklyn featured one of the largest scoreboards in baseball in 1914. It listed not only all of the FL games, but also Yankee, Giant, and, remarkably, Dodger games. Boys crawled on the rear structure to insert the proper numbers in slots. Similar boards were popular in the majors for several decades. (*Photo courtesy of UPI*)

Louis Browns were the dominant club in the league, but Byrne took advantage of a schism between the owner and his players to pry several Browns' stars to Brooklyn and in 1889 won the AA pennant. However, the start of the season was anything but auspicious. That old wooden park bugbear, fire, struck Washington Park. On May 23, the grandstand was mysteriously destroyed by a fire that broke out sometime after 9:30 P.M. when the players of amateur teams that were using the field had departed. Some $18,000 in damage was incurred, and the double-decked stand, which cut straight behind the plate, was almost totally destroyed. A new single-level stand was shortly erected in its place despite the fact that insurance produced only $7,000 for the club. The old stand held 2,600, the new 3,000. It was available before the Decoration Day doubleheader. The new stand was forty-eight feet longer than its predecessor, built in a crescent shape behind the plate. It was of a truss construction, which eliminated the support poles and was made with bolts holding it together. This, in the view of Byrne and club secretary Charles Ebbets, would enable them to move the stand if they decided to change venue.

Despite all of the problems engendered by the fire, 1889 was a banner year. Brooklyn won the AA pennant and drew 353,690 fans into Washington Park. The biggest draw was the Browns who attracted 95,395 in their eight games at Brooklyn. The Brooklyn club moved into the post-season series against the National League champions—none other than the New York Giants. Although the Giants won the series, Byrne recognized the value of being in the same league as Brooklyn's hated rival. During the off-season he began maneuverings that led him to jump from the AA into the NL for the 1890 season. Although he still had three years to run on the original ten-years Washington Park lease, Byrne decided to move to a new park—Eastern Park in the East New York section.

However, the Players League war broke out that season, and the PL entered a Brooklyn club into its circuit. The other American Association owners, furious with Byrne for deserting them with a championship team, formed a club of their own and put an AA team into Brooklyn as well. The scramble for playing sites was on. Wendell Goodwin, president of the PL team, and his partner George W. Channcey, got Eastern Park. Over the years, Byrne had played some games at Ridgewood Park, mostly on Sundays since the city of Brooklyn didn't permit Sunday play at Washington Park. The AA club grabbed Ridgewood. That left Byrne stuck in Washington Park. But he still had the best club.

A gala occasion was arranged on Monday, April 28, for the first NL game ever played in Brooklyn at Washington Park. The grandstand was decorated with flags and bunting, bands played, and Brooklyn blasted Philadelphia 10–0. But the opening was delayed three times by rain and only 2,870 fans (including 361 guests) showed up.

Of course, it also rained on the PL. The opening Players League game was the same day, and an even smaller crowd showed up at Eastern Park for Brooklyn's 3–1 win over the Philadelphia PL team. The formal opening at Eastern Park was held over until Wednesday, April 30, when some 4,000 fans saw Brooklyn beat New York 10–5. But the PL club had its problems, too. Late in the season attendance for John

Montgomery Ward's club dropped off sharply and shifted toward Byrne's NL team as they drove toward their second straight pennant. On September 8 the contractor who built the stands at Eastern Park placed a lien against the grandstand for $5,000. Ward and president Goodwin claimed that a subcontractor ordered the bill not paid and they, as a result, couldn't pay it. But when the final PL game was played at Eastern Park on September 12, they were more than happy to be finished with the financially disastrous 1890 season. During the winter the Players League folded. But Goodwin, being a decent businessman, made Byrne a proposition that enabled him to have the superior stand at Eastern Park and got Goodwin out from under some of his obligations.

The AA club, born in anger, died in apathy. Trying to get a jump on the other two teams, the AA entry

After they bought the Brooklyn FL franchise, the Ward brothers of baking fame set out to rebuild Washington Park. This view, taken in late March 1914, shows the job site a month before the scheduled opening of the FL season. The opener was delayed an additional month. (*Photo courtesy of UPI*)

The angular construction of Ebbets Field (above) shows itself as the teams line up for the National Anthem prior to the Dodger home opener against Boston in 1919. Fans in the boxes behind the plate were exposed to hard fouls in the days before protective screening. It paid to stay alert to the game. (*Photo courtesy of UPI*)

The exterior of Ebbets Field remained largely unchanged down through the forty-five years of its operation. The intersection shown here was then known as Sullivan Place and Cedar Place. Cedar Place, running towards left field, became McKeever Place in honor of the two brothers who built the building. Both later served as Dodger presidents. (*Photo courtesy of UPI*)

opened its season at Ridgewood Park on Thursday, April 17. About 2,000 fans were on hand as the Syracuse Stars beat the local club 3–2. The next day Brooklyn got even in a comedy of errors, 22–21, but Syracuse got the finale, 18–12. The opening day crowd was the largest of the home season for the hapless Brooklyn AA team and by midseason it folded, mired deep in the standings and red ink. Nicknamed the Gladiators, the AA club got thumbs-down from the Brooklyn fans.

The Dodgers moved into Eastern Park in 1891 and started by blowing all three games of the opening series to the Giants, including a 6–5 loss on opening day in which the Giants got the two decisive runs in the ninth. The start was an augury of a season that saw Boston win the pennant and Brooklyn sag to sixth. From 1891 to 1898 the Dodgers finished as high as third only once and flopped to tenth in the twelve-team NL in 1898.

Eastern Park was not entirely satisfactory to Byrne and, in 1892, he remodeled the stands. Everything was completely repainted, a new pavilion was built, the entrances to the bleachers changed, and an attractive walkway under the main grandstand added. The new arrangement provided for bleacherites to enter to the left after coming into the park; the "grandstand aristocrats," as one writer called them, went to the right; and the general admission fans straight ahead, following a path under the main grandstand. But Byrne was familiar enough with the habits of the Brooklyn bleacher cranks to install a picket fence between them and the grandstand.

In January 1898 Byrne died and Ebbets became the president of the club. Partly because of the $7,500 annual rent and partly because of poor attendance, Ebbets shifted the Dodgers back to the more conveniently located Washington Park between Fourth and Fifth avenues on Third Street. He also made an alliance with Baltimore's Ned Hanlon to strengthen the weak Brooklyn club. Jumping from its tenth-place finish in 1898, the Dodgers, under Hanlon, won the NL flag in 1899 and again in 1900. Ebbets had signed a fifteen-year lease for Washington Park, but he was to leave there before its expiration. The last phase of existence for Washington Park came during the Federal League war of 1914 to 1915.

Ebbets wound down the curtain on NL baseball in Washington Park on October 5, 1912. The Giants edged across one run in the seventh on Pat Ragon and made it stand up for a 1–0 victory in the finale. Over

10,000 attended what they knew was the final game in the old wooden park, and Shannon's Regimental Band provided mood music for the occasion. After the game many fans wandered around on the field taking a last look at the park. A good number spoke with Ebbets and expressed the hope that the team would play better in the new home. He said he hoped it would, too.

But Washington Park got a somewhat surprising renewal on life. The Ward brothers of baking fame bought a team in the outlaw Federal League and decided to have it play at the old NL park, since most fans were very familiar with it. However, it was completely reconstructed by the Wards into a brick and cement building with some structural steel foundation. A twelve-foot-high brick wall was built around the entire park, the stands were almost completely rebuilt on poured concrete, and the center-field bleachers were given a brick foundation. The first concrete was poured for the main grandstand on April 17, and George S. Ward announced that the park would be ready for a May 9 opening. The right-field stands were poured shortly thereafter. But the FL season had opened on April 13 in Baltimore, and Brooklyn was entirely a road club. After eight weeks of frantic work and $250,000, Washington Park was ready. Even then, however, the opening had to be put off until Monday, May 11. Brooklyn borough president Pound threw out the first ball, but Pittsburgh jumped on Tom Seaton for two first-inning runs and beat the home club 2–0. The crowd of nearly 15,000 made the opening something of a success but less than two years later Robert B. Ward, the prime mover in the Brookfed scheme, died. On September 30, 1915, Washington Park closed its doors for good.

Ebbets Field

On the night of September 24, 1957, the curtain came down on over a century of organized baseball competition in Brooklyn. Included in the crowd of 6,673 was a handful of the curious and sentimental, but for the most part the end was anything but auspicious. The Dodgers salvaged something—pride perhaps—by beating Pittsburgh 3–0 before the lights went out for the last time.

Before being converted into a housing development, rather unfortunately named Ebbets Field Apartments, the ballpark that had unceremoniously closed that night probably had been for more than four decades the most famous field in baseball. The performance of championship teams during its first and final decades was rather submerged by the raucous capacity of its fans and the fabled malfeasance of Dodger teams in intervening years.

Literally hundreds of stories, many of them apocryphal, are told of Brooklyn outfielders being skulled by pedestrian fly balls, baserunners piling up in wondrous profusion at third base, and various other misadventures. Of course, a good proportion of these stories happen to be true.

But it wasn't so much the on-field doings that gave Ebbets Field its enduring stamp of affection. It was the fans and the ballpark itself. The uninhibited performance of the patrons made a day at Ebbets Field an occasion to remember, and the eccentricities of the building made a wild adventure out of the best-played games. Among the more colorful Dodger rooters were the famous Hilda Chester with her "Hilda is Here" sign and clanging cowbell, and that catch-as-catch-can "orchestra" known as the Dodger Sym-phonie.

Ebbets Field was not built to be an eccentricity. When constructed, under the personal direction of Charles Ebbets, the ballpark was hailed as a palace of the game. Before the 1912 season, with two years still remaining on his lease at Washington Park, Ebbets decided to move out. He began buying land, with as much secrecy as a man could have in the folksy Brooklyn environment, in the Pigtown district of Flatbush, then largely inhabited by Italian immigrant families. He finally completed a block bounded by Montgomery Street, Bedford Avenue, Cedar Place, and Sullivan Place.

Then came the announcement, during the 1912 season, that a magnificent new home was in the offing for the Dodgers. The plans were released to the sportswriters of the four Brooklyn daily newspapers. They showed, among other things, an elaborate entrance rotunda on the Cedar and Sullivan corner that featured inlaid tile decoration in a baseball motif. The concrete and steel ballpark for Brooklyn was, indeed, designed to be spectacular.

It was then that the bizarre happenings that were to become characteristic of Ebbets Field began. Among the things *not* shown in the plans for the park was a press box. However, this fact didn't become evident until the field was opened the following season—long after the sports editors had unanimously praised the original plans. Embarrassment all around. The press facility was quickly added, and those who labored within it during the following forty-five seasons would bear eager testimony to its afterthought character.

Such a launching for the new baseball palace may have been an augury of things to come. But at the time the new park was more generally viewed as the impressive end product of a proud Brooklyn baseball heritage. Unfortunately, a preseason exhibition game was ensnarled when somebody forgot to bring the key to open the bleacher gate. Hell hath no fury like a Brooklyn fan unable to reach his bleacher seat. Another oversight included the American flag.

Somewhat shaken, Ebbets got the new park open. But what was happening behind the scenes was to have a far greater long-range effect on the course of Brooklyn baseball history than any momentary foul-ups on the field, no matter how disconcerting they might have been at the time. The new park cost substantially more than Ebbets had anticipated. In order to get it completed, he gave a half-interest in the club to the two brothers who owned the construction company that was building it, Steve and Ed McKeever. Both subsequently served as presidents of the club after Ebbets's death, and Cedar Place became known as McKeever Place in their honor.

On opening day Ebbets Field was minus the left-field stands that were to make it a death valley experience for left-handed picturers in later years. In fact, the left-field foul line extended exactly 418 feet 9 inches before it came to the wall. In the mid 1920s Ebbets put a small open-air bleacher with a concrete base in left, cutting the distance to 383 feet 8 inches. In the 1930s the double-deck stand was added, chopping the left-field line down to 353, and subsequent alterations reduced it to the 348 feet it was when the park closed. Willie Mays may have felt constrained in Ebbets Field, but Zack Wheat, Hall of Fame outfielder for the 1916 and 1920 championship Dodgers, didn't.

The original stands were double-deck from the right-field corner on Bedford Avenue around to just past third base on the Cedar Place side. There they met a concrete bleacher section which extended to the left-

In game four of the World Series, October 8, 1949, Bobby Brown of the Yankees has just rapped a triple to right field. Scoring on the play are Tommy Henrich, Yogi Berra, and Joe DiMaggio. Brook pitcher Joe Hatton, who replaced Don Newcombe, watches Brown's fifth-inning drive sail toward the Ebbets Field wall. (*Photo courtesy of UPI*)

Close-up of the first right-field scoreboard at Ebbets Field. After World War II it was modified somewhat and the famous Schaefer Beer sign was mounted on the top. But Abe Stark always remained, urging hitters to aim for his sign and win the free suit a bull's-eye produced. (*Photo courtesy of UPI*)

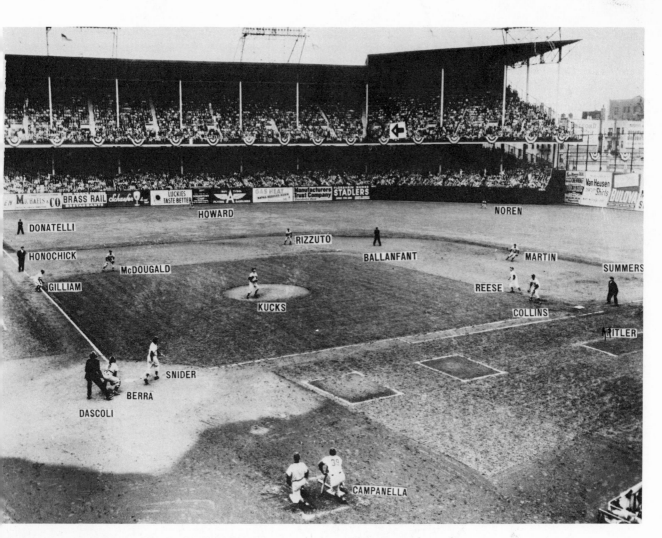

In the words of announcer Vin Scully, "To the screen . . . and gone." Duke Snider socks a three-run homer over the screen onto Bedford Avenue in the fourth game of the 1955 Series. Brooklyn won the game, 8–5, and captured its first (and last) World Championship in the seventh game at Yankee Stadium. (*Photo above courtesy of UPI; scorecard and newspaper on next page from Shannon Collection*)

(LEFT)
Here's the famous right-field wall at Ebbets Field from the outside. The crowd on Bedford Avenue is waiting the sale of standing-room bleacher tickets for the 1952 World Series. While waiting, they built up energy for the riot of noise that turned Ebbets Field into a baseball bedlam during games. (*Photo courtesy of Wide World*)

field wall on Montgomery Street. The walls around the park were about 9 feet high. Right field, however, always had a cozy feel to it. At no time in the park's history did the right-field corner extend more than 301 feet from the plate, and for almost all of its time it was less than that by 4 or 5 feet. Initially, center field was a healthy 476 feet 9 inches from the plate, a fact that would surprise many a later-day visiting pitcher. But it, too, gradually crept closer to home, as it were, until it was 389 feet away.

Ironically, the magnificent entrance rotunda with its artful mosaics turned out to be an enormous bottleneck. Once inside its circular grasp, fans had to fight one another to get in through the correct entrance to the park proper and find their seats. But even in its dingy death throes it retained an aura of faded glamour never to be forgotten.

Unforgettable, too, were some of the events of Ebbets Field. World Series games by the bushel. The Dodgers won pennants in 1916, 1920, 1941, 1947, 1949, 1952, 1953, 1955, and 1956—all of their games being played at Ebbets Field. Many memorable ones included the 1947 game in which Cookie Lavagetto's double in the ninth not only broke up a no-hit bid by the Yankees' Bill Bevans, but beat him, 3–2, in the bargain.

Cincinnati

Cincinnati has a long and interesting baseball history. Its ballparks have played a key role in that history. During the wooden ballpark era, Cincinnati had its share of shifts, fire, and highlights. The birthplace of professional baseball, Cincinnati spawned the fabulous Red Stockings in 1869. President Aaron Champion took much of his pride in the fact that the team toured across the country and beat all comers. But it did have a home. The original Reds played in a small park located where Lincoln Park is now, adjacent to Union Terminal.

When the National League was organized in 1876, it was natural for Cincinnati to have a club. The NL team played in the Avenue Grounds, located on Spring Grove Avenue near Arlington Street, and remained there until 1879. In 1880 the team moved to the Bank Street Grounds at the corner of Bank Street and Western Avenue.

Poor performance and poor attendance led the Reds to drop out of the National League after 1880, and there was no organized league team in the city in 1881. One season without their baseball was enough for the good burghers of Cincinnati. They started agitation for another NL franchise. When it didn't appear to be forthcoming, they joined in the movement that led to the formation of the American Association as a rival of the NL.

The new AA team started up in 1882 right where its predecessor NL club had finished, the Bank Street Grounds. They might have been there yet except for some clumsy management. The Union Association came into the field in 1884 and decided to place a club in Cincinnati. Nobody in the AA paid much heed to the new organization until they discovered that the UA had taken over the Bank Street Grounds' lease.

Evicted from his own ballpark by the rival Unions, a mortified club president Aaron Stern picked the best site he could find in a hurry, an old brickyard on Western Avenue at Findlay. The AA quickly constructed a park there and opened the 1884 season. Baseball was played there continuously until 1970. But the hastily constructed stands partially collapsed on opening day, May 1, causing one death and several injuries. The gleeful Unions immediately sought to have Mayor Stephens declare the new park unsafe. But Stephens sidestepped the issue and, in fact, struck down a planned exhibition by boxing champion John L. Sullivan at one of the Union games on the Bank Street Grounds.

The Reds recovered from the opening-day disaster and, though unable to repeat their 1882 AA pennant, remained one of the circuit's strongest clubs. In 1892, they moved into the NL.

Now permanently settled on the Western and Findlay site, the Reds decided to reconstruct the grandstand in 1894 and, in the process, turned the field around. Previously, the first-base line had run along Western Avenue; now the field faced Western so that the street was behind the right- and center-field parts of the park. The scheduled first opening day for the new grandstand was a gala occasion in Cincinnati, and Ohio Governor William McKinley was slated to throw out the first ball. But the game was rained out. When it was finally played on

Larry MacPhail brought night baseball to the major leagues in Crosley Field in 1934. However, the idea was tried out in Cincinnati as early as 1908 when the old wooden grandstand of Redland Field was still being used. (*Photos courtesy of UPI; aerial view pages 76–77 courtesy of UPI*)

Friday, April 20, Cincinnati beat the Cubs, 10–6, without McKinley, who two years later was elected president.

In 1901 the grandstand burned down. It was replaced by an ornate colonnade-style stand that was reminiscent of the 1893 Chicago World's Fair architecture then in vogue. It was nicknamed "Palace of the Fans" by the local press.

The park, actually the old park remade, was called Redland Field, a title that was to stick with the Cincinnati ballpark until 1934, when it became Crosley Field. Redland Field tended to accentuate some already growing local traditions. One was the sale of beer. Cincinnati, being a heavily German city, had a strong tradition of beer at the ballpark. This tradition had helped foster the growth of the old American Association, since the NL of the 1880s discouraged beer and liquor sales in its parks while the AA expressly permitted it at local option for the clubs involved.

In the new Redland Field waiters vended beer in mugs along "rooter's row," forerunner of boxes, which ran around behind the plate from first base to third. The beer wasn't considered much of a bargain then: It sold at twelve mugs for one dollar. Whether it was the beer, the ballpark, or the new grandstand, the Reds won twenty of the first twenty-five games at Redland Field. But they didn't fare as well either on the road or anywhere during the second half of the season and finished fourth.

Cincinnati didn't even challenge for a pennant during the next decade, but baseball remained a strong attraction and attendance was good. The club was then controlled by the Fleischman (yeast and gin) interests with local politician Boss Cox among other members of the owning group. In 1911 Gerry Herrmann took over as president for the group. The same year, the wooden stands at Redland Field were destroyed by fire.

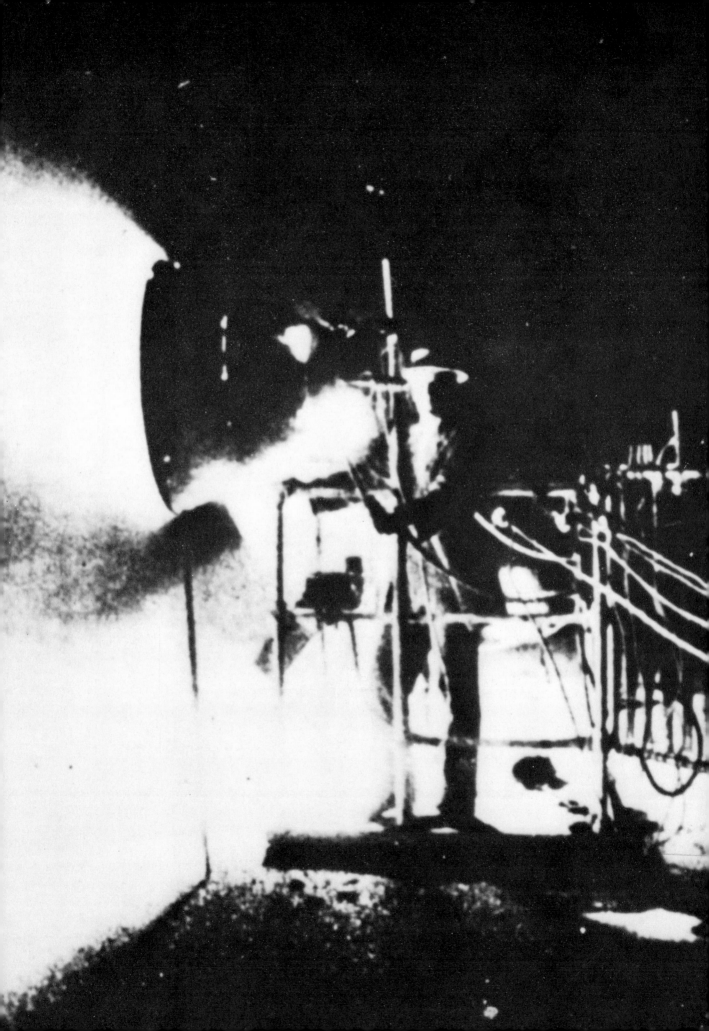

Crosley Field

Gerry Herrmann did more than pick up the pieces after Redland Field burned down in 1911. He decided to replace the wooden ballpark with one of the new concrete and steel designs, thus steering the Reds into a channel that was to influence their destiny for six decades. Herrmann handed the job of producing the new concrete Redland Field over to Harry Hake. Hake was ultimately to design all of the enlargements, additions, and improvements in the park for forty years.

The first game was played in the new park in April with all of the hoopla that traditionally attends to opening day in Cincinnati. A formal dedication was held on May 18, 1912. Interestingly, two American League dignitaries attended the formal ceremonies. Redland Field became one of the few ballparks ever to be dedicated by the presidents of both leagues. Ban Johnson, president of the AL, and Charles Comiskey, owner of the Chicago White Sox, were both on hand because of their personal history with the Cincinnati club. Johnson was once a newspaperman in Cincinnati, and Comiskey had managed the Reds in the 1890s. The original dimensions of the park were spacious: 360 feet down each line and 420 to center field.

In 1919 the famed Black Sox scandal brought Charles Comiskey back to Cincinnati for one of the most fateful episodes in his long and eventful baseball career. It was also the year that Hod Eller pitched the first no-hitter in the park.

Redland Field had been open for nine seasons when a ball was first hit out of it. Pat Duncan accomplished the feat on June 2, 1921, when he hit a ball over the fence in left.

Hake made the first of his extensive renovations in 1925 when the park was expanded, adding 5,000 seats to the capacity, mostly through the addition of field boxes. This type of addition cut down on the distances to the outfield walls. The field was also slightly turned, and the plate moved out 20 feet. The new dimensions were 339 feet to the left-field corner, 407 to center, and 377 to right down the line.

Redland Field achieved one of its historic distinctions in 1929, when the first radio broadcasts of major league baseball were made from it. Bob Burdette was behind the mike for the originating station, WLW of Cincinnati. Many clubs in the majors had deliberately avoided radio because the owners believed that people would stay home and listen to the broadcasts. The same argument was to be invoked a decade later against television, which began at Brooklyn's Ebbets Field. Time has demonstrated that these arguments may be valid for many attractions but are largely vacuous for baseball.

In 1933 Larry MacPhail came on the scene as part of the front office management of the Reds, and in February 1934 he convinced Powell Crosley, a local industrialist, to purchase the club. At this point Crosley Field assumed the name it was to carry through the rest of its existence.

MacPhail and Crosley made the next significant change in Cincinnati's baseball habits. They installed lights. Ironically, Cincinnati had been the site of an experimental night baseball game between two teams from local BPOE (Elks) Lodges in 1909 when portable lights were mounted on the wooden stands. MacPhail, however, became the first man to schedule regular major league games at night. During the first season, 1935, night games were limited by agreement to seven per season, one against each other team in the National League. On May 24, the first big league night game was played and the master switch that turned on the power plant was thrown by President Franklin D. Roosevelt in Washington, D.C., amid massive nationwide publicity.

Four days later the career of Babe Ruth ended at Crosley Field. For decades the park had an inclined terrace in front of the left-field wall. In early days many wooden parks had terraces to accommodate rows of fans in the outfield. On opening day in Cincinnati, even after the concrete stands were built, the Reds put temporary stands on the left-field terrace. Thus it remained as an anomaly in Crosley Field. Ruth, chasing a fly ball, stumbled and fell going up the incline. His pride damaged, he walked off the field. Ruth, finishing his career with the Boston Braves, never played another major league game.

Crosley Field disappeared for all intents in 1937, when the Mill Creek flood in January put the park under twenty-one feet of water. Two pitchers, Lee Grissom and Gene Schott, got in a rowboat and floated over the center-field wall for the benefit of wire service photographers, who syndicated the picture nationally.

The World Series returned to Cincinnati for the first

Crosley Field begins its next-to-last lap of existence when a wrecker's ball crashes against the right-field wall. The emblem for the 100th anniversary of professional baseball, dating from the Cincinnati Red Stockings of 1869, provides a convenient target. (*Photo courtesy of UPI*)

After the city of Cincinnati purchased Crosley Field, it was used as a pound for cars towed from illegal parking areas. Subsequently, the park was demolished but then largely reconstructed by a Reds fan on his property across the Ohio River in Kentucky. (*Photo left from Shannon Collection; photo below courtesy of UPI*)

ime in twenty years in 1939. Paced by the pitching of Bucky Walters and Paul Derringer and the hitting of catcher Ernie Lombardi, the Reds won NL flags in 1939 and 1940. They lost the Series to the Yankees in 1939 but beat Detroit the next fall. By 1939 the dimensions had been altered again. After the upper decks were extended into both corners and the plate moved out another 20 feet, the field measured 328 feet to left, 387 to straightaway center, and 366 into the right-field corner. It was generally to retain these dimensions until its closing. On several occasions temporary fences and screens were erected in right field to cut the distance to the corner. In 1946 a screen was placed in front of the bleacher sundeck, cutting the homerun distance to 342. It was taken down on June 30, 1950. A similar screen was installed in 1953, again cutting the distance to 342 in right, and removed before the 1959 season.

Other minor changes took place at Crosley Field over its final twenty years, including the new electric scoreboard installation in 1957 and complete resodding of the park in 1963. But basically it changed but little from 1938 to 1970 when the final game was played on June 24 against the Giants, the only club to hold an edge over the Reds there.

The capacity of Crosley Field seldom exceeded 30,000 throughout all of its changes and during its final years (1960 to 1970) it was 29,603. During most of its life Crosley Field had a unique environment. The laundry behind the wall in left field, Superior Towel and Linen Service, became almost as well known as the park itself. Atop the laundry was a large advertising sign. Part of it said "Hit this and win a Siebler suit." Before the sign was torn down, Wally Post of the Reds had won eleven suits and Willie Mays of the Giants, seven.

It was one of the major league's earliest night games that produced perhaps the most bizarre Crosley Field story. On July 31, 1935, the Reds played St. Louis. The game drew probably the largest crowd in Crosley Field history, though no accurate figures are available. Fans spilled onto the field. In all of the confusion, a girl named Kitty Burke snatched the bat out of Babe Herman's hands and ran up to the plate as a batter. Ushers escorted her away, but Miss Burke later toured in vaudeville as "the only girl ever to bat in the major leagues."

Riverfront Stadium

During their final years at Crosley Field, the Reds developed a consistent contender under Sparky Anderson. In 1970 the team moved into a new home in downtown Cincinnati called Riverfront Stadium. This circular park with its almost bull ring ambience, was treated to a World Series at the end of its first season and again two years later. The Reds were also engaged in interdivisional post-season playoffs with the Mets in 1973.

Riverfront Stadium was a boon to the Reds' attendance, which had passed one million only four times from 1912 to 1969 in Crosley Field. In 1970 the Reds drew 567,937 in their final thirty-four games at Crosley and 1,235,631 in forty-three dates at Riverfront, setting a season club record of 1,803,568. That record was broken by the 2,017,601 in 1973. During the first four-plus years of operation, Riverfront never lost a game to rain.

Occupying a forty-eight-acre site near downtown Cincinnati, Riverfront Stadium has built-in parking levels below the field grade. It was also the first park to use the small cutout or "sliding pit" concept rather than a full dirt infield with its synthetic surface.

Its 51,726 seats include 20,027 boxes of various types. It absorbed 175,000 cubic yards of concrete in its construction along with 10,000 tons of structural steel and 13,000 tons of reinforcing steel. Riverfront Stadium has colorful pastels in its multitiered levels which give the empty park the look of an artist's color sample.

Crosley Field, meanwhile, has been largely dismantled and reconstructed on his own property by a devoted Reds' fan from nearby Kentucky.

Riverfront Stadium is essentially built atop a giant parking garage; fans enter the park from underneath. The parking area will also be utilized for a new sports arena being built next door. In the background is the approach leading to the suspension bridge over the Ohio River into Kentucky. (*Photo courtesy of Cincinnati Reds*)

Cleveland

Cleveland, one of three charter members of the 1900 American League, was once a fixture in the National League. That NL Cleveland club brought Cy Young to the majors, produced a two-time NL batting champion, and in its final season recorded the worst record in the history of the NL.

J. Ford Evans and some other Clevelanders brought a club into the NL for the first time in 1879. The club, managed by pitcher Jim McCormick, came home sixth, while McCormick compiled the unique pitching record of twenty wins and forty defeats. McCormick did better in 1880 (45–28) and so did the team, advancing to third. From there until 1884 when it dropped out of the NL, the club never finished higher than fourth. Evans himself tried his hand at managing in 1882 but only got up to fifth place. His replacement as club president, C. H. Bulkley, then dismissed him.

After the city was out of organized baseball for a couple of years, two brothers, Frank D. and M. Stanley Robison, organized a Cleveland team in the American Association. They also built a new park for the club at East 68th Street and Lexington Avenue. After a sixth-place finish in the AA in 1888, the Robisons skipped into the NL and had a sixth-place club in the senior circuit in 1889. In 1890 they survived a challenge from a Players League club owned by Albert L. Johnson. That same year, Cy Young joined the Cleveland NL squad and posted a 13–12 record. In the years to follow, Young was to compile the highest total of victories in major league history, 511.

After the start of the 1891 season, the Robisons hired the former PL club manager Oliver (Pat) Tebeau to handle their team. Tebeau led the club to its highest heights in the NL, finishing second in 1892, 1895, and 1896, and third in 1893. Young hit his stride under Tebeau's handling, winning 36 games in 1892, 32 in 1893, and leading the league with a 35–10 record in 1895. Jess Burkett won the batting title in successive seasons, 1895 and 1896, with averages of .423 and .410.

Then the Robisons got an opportunity to gain control of the St. Louis franchise. When they did, they began to shift the top Cleveland talent to St. Louis. In 1899 Tebeau became the St. Louis manager, Young and Burkett going with him. The remainder of the Cleveland club, commonly called the Spiders, was handed over to Lave Cross to manage. The entire season was a farce. The Spiders lost a record 134 games in 1899, managing only 20 wins, also an all-time NL record. During that year, Cleveland posted losing streaks of 24, 16, and 14 games. The 24-game losing skein is still the NL standard for futility.

After mid-August, Cleveland played almost all of its games on the road and at the end of the season, it was one of the four clubs dropped by the NL.

In 1900 the newly renamed American League grabbed off the territory and the wooden ballpark. On opening day, the new AL club drew the largest crowd in Cleveland since 1897. By 1910 club president John Kilfoyl decided to join the concrete and steel ballpark movement begun the year before in Philadelphia and Pittsburgh. On April 21, 1910, League Park became the

The New York ballparks for decades . . . the Polo Grounds, Yankee Stadium, and Ebbets Field. It's the Giants at the Polo Grounds, but they're the ones in visiting gray this day as they play the Mets on June 6, 1962—Jack Sanford pitching to Felix Mantilla. Yankee Stadium shows its magnificent ambience from the lower deck in right field. Ebbets Field, baseball's riot of color and noise, watches as Yankee righty Bob Turley wheels toward the plate in the 1955 World Series. One of Ebbets Field's landmark interior features, the right-field scoreboard, is on the following page. (*Photos, top to bottom: George Kalinsky, George Kalinsky,* Sport *magazine; photo right courtesy of* Sport *magazine*)

...real hit ! Schaef

4 FT.

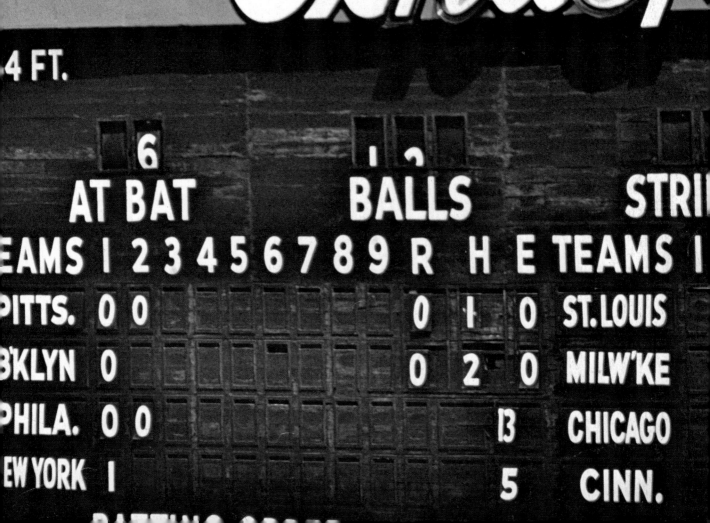

	6					
AT BAT		BALLS			STRI	

TEAMS	1	2	3	4	5	6	7	8	9	R	H	E	TEAMS	1
PITTS.	0	0								0	1	0	ST. LOUIS	
B'KLYN	0									0	2	0	MILW'KE	
PHILA.	0	0									13		CHICAGO	
EW YORK	1										5		CINN.	

The baseball lady in red,
Connie Mack Stadium, during
its final years. The Dagwood-
sandwich-style grandstand
behind the plate was fronted by
the unique see-through Plexi-
glas that replaced the usual
protective screen. The press box
is at the top. Lou Brock stands
at the ready in left field before
the stands Connie Mack added
to the park in 1925 as action
stirs in the Cardinals' bullpen.
Johnny Briggs of the Phillies
cuts loose a throw from right.
Brock heads home in the ninth
inning of a close game. The
high and handy walls in old
ballparks made every fly ball an
adventure. (*Photos courtesy of
Gerry Beatty*)

Aerial view of Comiskey Park after its transformation into White Sox Park and the neighborhood renovation that revived the park. New parking areas almost entirely surround the park and access was improved with the opening of the nearby Dan Ryan Expressway. (*Photo courtesy of Chicago White Sox*)

Fenway Park (*left*) and Forbes Field (*above*) were built within three years of each other, but Fenway outlasted its older brother. *Clockwise from upper left:* Baltimore's Memorial Stadium, Jarry Park in Montreal, Milwaukee County Stadium, and Cleveland Stadium. (*Photos left and above courtesy of Dave Hynes; photos below courtesy of Baltimore Orioles, Montreal Expos, Milwaukee Brewers, and Cleveland Indians*)

All that remain are the memories. The final games at Forbes Field (*below*) and Yankee Stadium (*right*) at least drew large and enthusiastic crowds of mourners and a few exhibitionists. Braves Field (*bottom*) expired in virtual silence and only its Gaffney Street side remains today as a mute testimony of its contribution to baseball lore. (*Photos below and bottom courtesy of Dave Hynes; photo right by George Kalinsky*)

League Park was the fourth concrete grandstand in baseball when it opened in 1910, but it became only a part-time home for the Indians after 1932 when the huge Municipal Stadium on the lakefront was built. The only World Series games played in League Park were in 1920 when the Indians beat the Dodgers. (*Photo courtesy of UPI*)

For fourteen years, Cleveland was the only team in the majors to use more than one park on a regular basis during the season. The Sunday, night, and holiday games were generally reserved for Municipal (now Cleveland) Stadium while weekday affairs were held at tiny League Park. (*Photos courtesy of UPI; photo page 88 also courtesy of UPI*)

Virtually all AL attendance records were set in the cavernous stadium on the shores of Lake Erie. The wind off the lake can make a spring or fall day a bitter experience for fans and players alike in this massive ballpark. (*Photo courtesy of UPI; photo next page courtesy of Cleveland Indians*)

fourth concrete and steel grandstand in the major leagues.

During the thirty-seven seasons it was used, League Park hardly changed perceptibly. It had a close, high wall in right field 290 feet from the plate, which was a prime target for extra base hits by lefty swingers though the wall was high enough to make homers at least more than a normal effort. League Park had a spacious center field, 450 feet or more. Down the line toward the bleachers in left field, it measured 376 feet to the corner.

League Park got its only exposure to the World Series in 1920. Playing under the cloud of the just revealed Black Sox scandal, the Indians and Brooklyn opened the best five-of-nine Series in Ebbets Field where Cleveland took the opener and the Dodgers the next two. Then the Series shifted to League Park. On October 9, Stan Coveleski earned his second win of the Series, 5–1, to tie the affair at two games apiece. The next day Jim Bagby, Sr., won, 8–1, and Cleveland won the crusher on October 11 when Duster Mails outpitched

Ted Williams hit only one inside-the-park homer in his entire career. He hit it here and it is easy to see why. Before the wire fence was built in center, distances ranged well beyond 450 feet to the stands, even in the power alleys. (*Photos courtesy of UPI*)

Sherry Smith, 1–0. With Cleveland now holding a four games to two edge, Coveleski closed out the Series with his third win, 3–0, on October 12.

Cleveland earned the distinction of being the only team in the major leagues to use two parks on a regular basis after 1932, when the huge Municipal Stadium was opened on the lakefront. Though they continued to play many games in League Park, their big night, Sunday, and holiday games were invariably played at Municipal Stadium, as it was then called.

League Park was more economical to operate but was the smallest park in the AL for many years, holding only 21,414. It did have a large proportion of boxes for a park of its era, but its uses were clearly limited.

League Park remained a daylight park, and when it was abandoned only three other parks in the majors were without lights. The Indians, of course, played their night games at Municipal Stadium beginning in 1939. When Bill Veeck became president of the Tribe in 1947, he moved the entire schedule into the big lakefront ballpark, and the Indians have played all of their games there since. In 1948 Lou Boudreau managed the Indians to their first pennant in almost three decades. Combined with Veeck's promotions (orchids for the ladies, a laundry in the ballpark, gimmicks and giveaways), the winning team attracted a season total of 2,620,627 which included a day game crowd of 74,181 and a night game turnout of 78,382. All three are still AL records.

The bowl-shaped Cleveland Stadium was first used on an occasional basis by the Indians. Since it has come into regular use, its dimensions have been around 320 feet down each line and 410 to center. Originally, the center-field figure was much deeper, but a screen around the outfield established the stable figure.

Al Lopez managed the Indians to another flag in 1954, breaking a five-year Yankee streak. During the late 1940s and early 1950s, Cleveland had many outstanding players including Luke Easter, Dale Mitchell, Jim Hegan, and Larry Doby, the first AL black player. But since the days of Cy Young, pitching has been the hallmark of Cleveland clubs. The pennant-winning teams featured such greats as Bob Feller, Bob Lemon, Mike Garcia, and Early Wynn. The four-game sweep by the New York Giants in the 1954 World Series was such a stunning surprise for just that reason. In recent years, Cleveland has had uninspiring teams and corresponding attendance figures.

Detroit

If a fielder trips over a cobblestone while running down a ball in Tiger Stadium, you can blame the park's ancestry for it. The site of what is called Tiger Stadium has been the only one used for American League games in Detroit since the league's formation in 1900. Prior to becoming a ballpark, the area was the site of the Haymarket and was paved with cobblestones. The chances of one turning up today are virtually nil since the park has gone through so many transformations, but you never know. In any case, it would be a unique excuse for failure to field the ball.

Actually, Detroit's baseball history goes back beyond the American League. The city had a championship team in the National League in 1887 and participated in a unique postseason World Series.

When Cincinnati was expelled from the NL after the 1880 season, a Detroit club was accepted to replace the Ohioans. William Thompson was the club president and Frank Bancroft, who was to win an NL pennant at Providence in 1884, was the field manager. But in the two seasons that Bancroft managed it, the team struggled to play .500 ball. In 1883 Bancroft shuffled off to Providence, and John Chapman became the manager. Things immediately got worse. The club was seventh, winning forty of its ninety-eight games. Chapman stayed another year. The club dropped to eighth, winning twenty-eight and losing eighty-four. Chapman went. The new club president, Joseph Marsh, wanted action. Charlie Morton started the 1885 season as the manager,

but Bill Watkins replaced him during the campaign. Watkins was to remain until the club disbanded at the end of the 1888 season.

After the 1885 season, Detroit swung one of that era's biggest trades. It purchased Dennis (Big Dan) Brouthers, Hardy Richardson, Jack Rowe, and Deacon White from Buffalo's NL club for $8,500. It was one of baseball's biggest bargains of any era. The so-called Big Four immediately produced sensational seasons, and Detroit jumped to second in 1886. Brouthers was one of the best hitters of his time, winning batting crowns in one or another major league in 1882, 1883, 1889, 1890, and 1891. The 1886 club won eighty-seven and lost only thirty-six, recording the highest percentage in team history, .707. But Chicago was 90–34 and won the pennant. In 1887 Detroit took the flag. After the season, the club started out on a cross-country World Series against the St. Louis Browns, the American Association champions, which encompassed fifteen games in nine different cities. Only games three and thirteen were played in Detroit. But the home team won both (2–1 and 6–3) and took the Series, 10–5.

After the fifth-place finish of 1888, Detroit dropped out of the National League and was replaced by the Cleveland team, which jumped from the AA.

Following the demise of the AA, the old Western Association was reorganized into the Western League with Ban Johnson as its president. This circuit served ultimately as the nucleus for the AL. Detroit was a

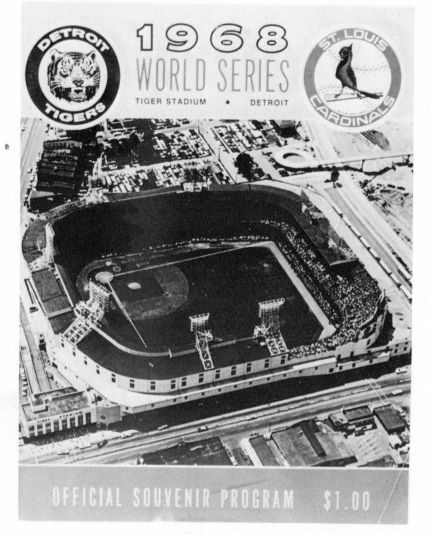

Although the Detroit ballpark is now known as Tiger Stadium after several reconstructions, it is the same park that was familiar to previous generations as Navin Field and Briggs Stadium. The wooden Bennett Park was on the same site. (*Scorecard from Shannon Collection*)

member throughout the transitional period. But the first AL game ever played in Detroit was hardly a sensation for the local fans. It was a no-hitter on opening day, April 19, 1900, by Morris (Doc) Amole of Buffalo. The early Detroit AL clubs played most of their games in Bennett Park, whose wooden grandstand held 8,500 fans. When Frank Navin became president of the team in 1911, Ty Cobb was already a superstar, and Navin decided to build a new park.

The Tigers had three straight AL pennants in 1907, 1908, and 1909. Navin had no reason to believe that they might not continue to win championships, and he sought to be in a position to benefit financially if they did. Thus a new concrete and steel grandstand was constructed for the 1912 season, and Tiger Stadium was born. It was, in the custom of the day, called Navin Field. Unfortunately for Navin, the Tigers didn't win another pennant until 1934. In the meantime, Navin Field with its 29,000 capacity wasn't often strained. The dimensions of the original concrete park were lopsided against left-hand hitters. The original right-field line measured 370 feet (plus 10 15/16 inches) and the left-field corner was 345. Center field was a spacious 467 feet. Some reconstruction shaved left field down to 340 during the 1920s.

Navin died in 1935 and Walter O. (Spike) Briggs became president of the Tigers, who had won the 1934 and 1935 AL titles. Briggs set out to expand the park again, from its capacity of 38,000 when he took over to more than 50,000. The reconstruction took place in time for the opening of the 1938 season and saw the new stands in right cut the corner from 372 down to 325 where it remains today. The capacity grew from 38,000 to 54,900.

The Tigers won more pennants in 1940 and 1945, principally around the long-ball slugging of Hank Greenberg and some outstanding pitching by Hal Newhouser, Schoolboy Rowe, and Dizzy Trout.

When Briggs died, his son, Walter O. Briggs, Jr., took control of the Tigers until 1956. When John Fetzer became president of the club in 1960, he decided to change the name of the park and on January 1, 1961, it became Tiger Stadium.

Despite its relatively large size, Tiger Stadium gives an intimate feeling. This is largely due to the surrounding of the field by double-decked stands all around the outfield, including center field. The stands are covered in all parts of the park except deep center, where there is an opening in the roof. The main scoreboard is above the open stands in the upper deck in center field.

Tiger Stadium is devoid of advertising on its walls, at least partly because those walls are screens in front of the stands around the outfield, which are virtually at field level in almost all parts of the park. This proximity to the players gave rise to one of the ugliest incidents in World Series history in 1934. The Tigers played St. Louis, and Enos (Country) Slaughter of the Cardinals was ordered from a game when he was showered with garbage in left field. The fans were angered by a hard slide into third by Slaughter, and Commissioner Landis removed him from the game for what the Commissioner called Slaughter's own protection. The infuriated Cardinals won the Series, four games to three.

Tiger Stadium earned a historical footnote of a pleasanter kind by being the last American League ballpark to have lights installed in it. The first night game in Detroit wasn't played until June 15, 1948, when the Tigers beat the Philadelphia A's 4–1. Lights or no lights, Tiger fans have been among the most loyal in baseball and since 1944, the team has failed to draw one million or more only three times and hasn't gone below 800,000 since 1943. During that span, Detroit has won only one pennant (1968).

Houston

Perhaps the eighth wonder of the world—at least the wonder of the baseball world—is the Astrodome. Texans are prone to do things in a big way, and Houston certainly did it with the world's first indoor ballpark.

In 1961 several things happened in Houston that eventually resulted in the opening of the Astrodome four years later. First was the granting of a National League expansion franchise to the Texas city. On January 31 the voters of Harris County (in which Houston is situated) approved 18 million dollars in general obligation bonds for the construction of a domed stadium. Then construction was started on a ballpark to serve as the team's home on an interim basis while the domed stadium was being built.

Initially, the club was nicknamed the Colt .45s, and on opening day in 1962 the team made its debut in a 32,000-seat ballpark called Colt Stadium. During its three-year life as a major league park, Colt Stadium played host to 2,369,731 fans. In its first season of operation, 1965, the Astrodome attracted 2,151,470.

But Colt Stadium, an open-air, concrete affair, had some memorable moments before its brief career ended. The first two no-hitters in Texas major league history were pitched there, and both of them were thrown by Colt pitchers. The first came on May 17, 1963, when Don Nottebart turned the trick against the Phillies. But Nottebart, despite the no-hitter, failed to get a shutout. A fifth-inning error put Don Demeter aboard. He was sacrificed to third by Clay Dalrymple and scored on a sacrifice fly by Don Hoak. Carl Warwick

went four-for-four for Houston, including a homer and a triple. The next no-hitter came the following season. On April 23, 1964, Ken Johnson fired one against Cincinnati. While Nottebart won his game, 4–1, Johnson had an even more depressing experience. He lost 1–0 on an unearned run scored by Pete Rose in the ninth inning. Joe Nuxhall pitched a five-hitter and won for the Reds.

On December 22, 1962, the Harris County Commissioners Court went to the county voters for an additional 9.6 million dollars in bonds for the construction of the new domed stadium and the issue was carried, enabling the construction to be completed on schedule for the 1965 opening game. Only a couple of months before, Houston fans had given a vote of another kind when only 1,638 showed up—the smallest crowd in Houston history—for a Colt game against the hapless New York Mets at Colt Stadium on September 8, 1962.

When the Astrodome opened for business, some interesting discoveries were made. The roof was made of 4,796 separate panes of glass to allow the sun to shine through and make the grass grow. The sun reflected off the glass into the eyes of the fielders, making vision a near impossibility and seeing a fly ball out of the question. Besides, the grass died anyway. In typical Texas fashion, these problems were attacked with extreme vigor. The roof was coated over and sealed off so that light would not penetrate it. Then came a development that had more far-reaching effects.

The Chemstrand Division of Monsanto produced a

Houston has had two major league ballparks and they were directly across Kirby Street from one another. The original Colt Stadium (*above*) was built for the NL expansion club in 1962 while the Astrodome was being constructed. Somewhat spacious, Colt Stadium was a difficult park for homers. But that was partly by intent, since the early Colt .45s were hardly the long-ball terrors of the NL. As a team, the 1962 Colts hit 105 circuits, about half the total of league-leading San Francisco. The temporary Colt Stadium was demolished after the Astrodome opened in 1965 and the team name was changed to Astros. Harry Craft managed almost the entire three-year tour in Colt Stadium but never got to the Astrodome. He was fired midway through the 1964 season. (*Photos here and next page courtesy of Baseball Hall of Fame*)

unique synthetic turf that was tried as a solution to the grass problem. It worked, and baseball discovered the artificial surface. In honor of its original purpose, the new material was named AstroTurf. Since its installation in Houston, AstroTurf and other synthetic surfaces have been installed in virtually every new stadium built. AstroTurf is described as having the texture of a stiff nylon hairbrush. This is reasonable enough, since it is composed of strands of nylon and other fibers to a thickness of about half an inch and colored green for ballparks.

Another of the rather impressive things about the Astrodome is the scoreboard, erected at a cost in excess of 2 million dollars. It is the equivalent height of a four-story building, measures 474 feet across and weighs 300 tons. It contains, among other elements, 50,000 electric bulbs.

But without doubt the most impressive parts of the Astrodome are the sky boxes and sky suites. The boxes, located on the eighth level above the field, have a capacity of either twenty-four or thirty. Behind each is a suite, fully carpeted, which includes closed-circuit television, ice makers, telephones, refrigerators, restrooms, and catered hors d'oeuvres. Above the sky boxes is the roof which makes the Astrodome unique among ballparks. It has a clear span of 642 feet, double that of any other previous building. From the field, the roof is a maximum height of 208 feet straight up. An eighteen-story building could be built behind second base and fit comfortably inside the roof. At that, the field itself is 25 feet above the ground level outside the Astrodome.

One of the major reasons for building a domed stadium in Houston had nothing to do with the normal baseball bugaboo, rain. The rationale basically was to free the fans from the often oppressive heat and humidity in the area; and the enormous air-conditioning system which keeps the temperature at a constant 72 degrees does just that.

Befitting its rather unusual character, the Astrodome has had a couple of rather unusual games played in it. The most unique was undoubtedly the twenty-four-inning marathon between the Astros and the Mets on April 15, 1968. Tom Seaver started for the Mets against Don Wilson of Houston. Wilson went nine innings, allowing five hits. Seaver went ten innings and permitted only two hits. Neither came even close to figuring in the decision. Houston finally won, 1–0, concluding the longest extra-inning night game in baseball history and the longest 1–0 game by time ever played. Bill Rhor took the loss and Wade Blasingame got the win.

Wilson also had the honor of being the first Astro pitcher to get a shutout while pitching a no-hitter and, at the same time, pitch the first no-hitter in the Astrodome. He struck out fifteen men while beating Atlanta 2–0 on June 18, 1967. For the record, Richie Allen of the Phillies hit the first homerun in the Astrodome in an NL game on April 12, 1965. The home team didn't get a round-tripper until April 24, when Bob Aspromonte socked one off Vernon Law of Pittsburgh.

The Astrodome: the first indoor ballpark and the birthplace of AstroTurf. (*Photo courtesy of Houston Astros; photo next page courtesy of UPI*)

Jersey City

In 1955 Jersey City seemed like the remotest place on earth for National League baseball. But, as part of his effort to bring pressure on civic officials in New York for a new downtown Brooklyn stadium, Dodger president Walter F. O'Malley announced that the Dodgers would play seven home games in Roosevelt Stadium for the 1956 season.

For O'Malley's purpose of proving the Dodgers would play games somewhere besides Ebbets Field, Roosevelt Stadium was as good a choice as any and better than most. It was major league from the standpoint of playing dimensions, had one of the best minor league grandstands in the country (permanent capacity of 24,500), and had a long history of Triple-A International League baseball support.

On opening day, when Eddie Fisher showed up to sing the National Anthem, New York officials began to get a bit nervous—but evidently not nervous enough. Jersey City Mayor John J. Grogan—no dummy—waited until the third Dodger game at Roosevelt Sta-dium (on June 25) to throw out the ceremonial first ball. No chilling Jersey winds for him. In seven games that season, the Dodgers drew 148,371 fans, most of whom were old Giant rooters and lustily booed the Dodgers. The Jersey City IL club had been a Giant farm and it built Giant loyalty amongst Jersey City fans. They were rewarded on August 15, the last game of the Jersey City schedule, when the Giants beat the Dodgers, 1–0, on a two-hitter by Johnny Antonelli and a fourth-inning homer by Willie Mays.

All NL clubs, plus the Cleveland Indians in an exhibition, played at Roosevelt Stadium in 1956. The next season, the campaign opened and closed against the Phillies and the other six clubs came through for night games in between. In all, fifteen NL games were played at Roosevelt Stadium in two seasons and Brooklyn won eleven, but lost twice to the Giants in two tries. The games were the first for Jersey City in the majors since 1889, when the temporarily homeless Giants played their first two games at Oakland Park.

Kansas City

The history of Kansas City baseball is a long and varied one that threads through almost every league that ever operated on a major league basis—although the results were generally less than sensational.

Today, however, Kansas City has established itself as a major league city with a fascinating ballpark. The 40,672-seat Royals Stadium is the culmination of a chain of circumstances begun in 1884 when the Union Association placed a club in Kansas City. With a vacant ballpark lying around, the NL moved in for one year in 1886, and the sixth-place club perished without a trace.

The American Association gave Kansas City a try in 1888. When the eighth-place team of that year could only improve to sixth in 1889, the AA was gone from K.C. The AL had a club in the city during its charter season of 1900 and the eastern expansion of the following season took the city out of the majors again. The Federals gave it a try in 1914 and 1915, but the Cowboys went the way of the entire circuit.

Kansas City latched on hard to its minor league American Association franchise, which served for decades as one of the chief farm clubs for the New York Yankees during their days as baseball's most dominant team. Many Yankee greats, including Phil Rizzuto and

Municipal Stadium in Kansas City was rebuilt several times; it had variously been known as Ruppert Stadium and Blues Stadium when it was the home of the Triple-A American Association Blues. (*Photo courtesy of Kansas City Royals; photo on pages 110 and 112–113 also courtesy of Kansas City Royals*)

Mickey Mantle, spent some minor league time in the uniform of the Kansas City Blues. As a result of this talent flow, the Blues were able to win all or part of nine championships or playoff titles before leaving the AA after 1954 to make way for a major league club.

In 1923 the minor league club put up a ballpark that was gradually expanded to hold 17,476 by 1940. This park, located on 22nd Street at Brooklyn Avenue, was to serve as the home of baseball in Kansas City for half a century. Known for many years as Ruppert Stadium during the Yankee ownership, it became Blues Stadium and was sold to Chicago industrialist Arnold Johnson. A friend of Yankee co-owners Del Webb and Dan Topping, Johnson was gradually convinced by local sports editor Ernie Mehl that the park ought to have a big-league club in it and that Johnson should buy a team to move there.

Johnson bought the Philadelphia A's after the end of the 1954 season. He sold Blues Stadium to the city, and an immediate renovation and expansion job began. During a period of some twenty-two weeks, the old park was completely rebuilt and double-decked, raising its capacity to 32,561. The Philadelphia A's became the Kansas City A's.

On April 12, 1955, Kansas City celebrated its return to the majors with a gala party which overflowed the ballpark and spilled over into the entire city as the newly minted home club beat Detroit. Former President Harry Truman threw out the first ball at what was now known as Municipal Stadium amid an audience of mayors, governors, and other dignitaries. Also on hand was Connie Mack, the ninety-two-year-old former big league catcher, owner, and manager who had controlled the fortunes of the A's for fifty of their Philadelphia seasons, guiding them to nine AL pennants.

The city paid Arnold Johnson $500,000 for Blues Stadium and the right to rename it Municipal Stadium. Johnson then invested $100,000 of that to buy the scoreboard from Braves Field for the Kansas City park. Meanwhile, Johnson sold Connie Mack Stadium, which had been acquired along with the A's, to the Phillies on December 10, 1954, for $1,675,000.

When its renovation was completed, the new park in Kansas City resembled the former park, which served as the base for its construction, in only slight ways. The new outfield dimensions showed 331 feet down the left-field line, 421 feet to center, and 338 down the line in right. Over the years, Municipal Stadium was actually to grow larger in the outfield, somewhat in contrast to the normal trend for such things. By 1961 it was 370 feet to left and 353 to right.

During the Charlie Finley days in the sixties, goats (often dyed different colors) wandered around eating the grass on the hill between the right-field screen fence and the outer wall on Brooklyn Avenue. Sometimes, the goats had very little company. Attendance was over one million during each of the first two years in Kansas City, then began a steady downward drift. In 1967 the A's and Mr. Finley skipped off to Oakland where they again became great and famous as they had been in Philadelphia.

Political pressure mounted with explosive force in Kansas City and the states whose border it straddles, Kansas and Missouri. The 1969 expansion of the American League was to include a team for Kansas City. The new clubowner, Ewing Kauffman, signed a four-year lease on the old Municipal Stadium. But on June 27, 1967, the voters of Jackson County had approved 43 million dollars in bonds for the construction of the Harry S. Truman Sports Complex, which would have separate parks for the new Royals and the Kansas City Chiefs of the National Football League. Another 13 million dollars in bonds was required, and investments by the owners of the two clubs finally brought the total price tag on the complex to well over 70 million dollars.

But on April 10, 1973, it all came to fruition when the Royals played their home night opening game in the park, defeating Texas 12–1. For the first time, the fans saw their new marvel. Included in the wonders was the computer-operated, twelve-story, 16,320-bulb scoreboard shaped like the Royals' crownlike logo and a 1.5-million-dollar stadium club.

On July 21 a 322-foot-wide water spectacular joined the attractions at Royals Stadium. Unique in baseball, this water show runs from center field toward the right-field corner and contains a 10-foot high waterfall. The waterfall descends from an upper cascade pool. The pool, in turn, is a backdrop for two 40-foot wide water fountain pools. The entire business is illuminated by 670 500-watt lamps. In front of the waterworks are five 10-foot high horseshoe waterfalls. The complex contains 638 nozzles, requires about a half-million gallons

of water, and can fire fifty thousand gallons of water skyward at one time. The water show produces some 150 different light, color, and water effects.

If nothing else, the old song refrain still holds; and if things weren't up to date in Kansas City baseball before, they are now.

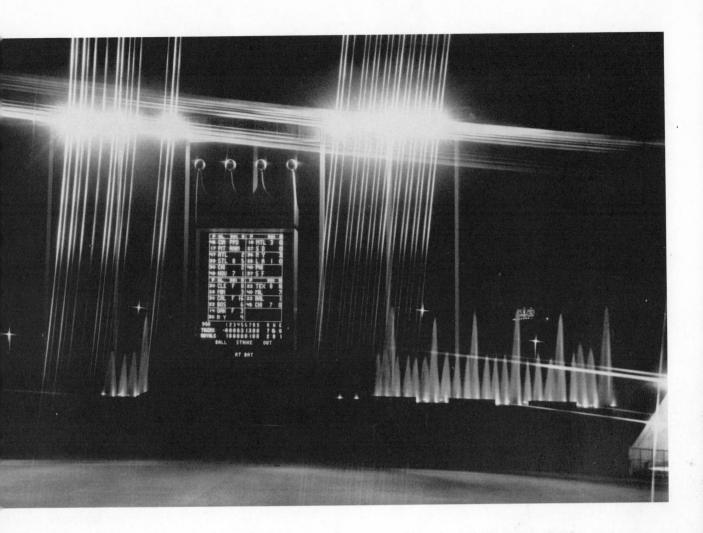

Royals Stadium is the first ballpark built expressly for baseball use since Dodger Stadium in 1962. It also includes
baseball's first permanent water show. The 1973 All-Star
Game here was only the second ever in Kansas City. The
first was the 1960 game at Municipal Stadium. (*Photo facing page courtesy of Kansas City Royals; photo above
courtesy of UPI*)

Los Angeles

Like most cities that spent the better part of this century outside of the major leagues, Los Angeles developed a firm root for minor league baseball. The city had two clubs for much of the time before it became big league: the Los Angeles Angels and the Hollywood Stars, two of the bulwark franchises of the Pacific Coast League.

It was for the original Angels that little Wrigley Field on 42nd Place at Avalon was built in 1930. It was used by them until 1957. It was an office for the Dodgers before Dodger Stadium opened and was home to the new Los Angeles Angels in the American League in 1961. Then it was owned by the city of Los Angeles and used by the recreation department for various youth activities in the largely black neighborhood that now surrounds it.

Gilmore Field in Hollywood was put up by Bob Cobb, Victor Ford Collins, and their associates when the old Mission club was switched from San Francisco to become the Hollywood Stars, initiating the west coast version of the then east coast Giant-Dodger rivalry. It has since vanished.

From these still celebrated parks much local baseball lore was spun which laid the foundation for the startling move of the Dodgers from Brooklyn to Los Angeles for the 1958 season. When the Dodgers arrived, they decided not to play in Wrigley Field, even though they owned it. Instead, they made a deal to use the cavernous Los Angeles Coliseum while their own new ballpark was under construction.

Thus the Coliseum built for the 1932 Olympic Games instantly became the largest baseball park in the world. On opening day, the first major league crowd in Los Angeles numbered a record 78,672 as the Giants and Dodgers renewed their acquaintance 2,500 miles from their ancestral homes.

During the four years that the Dodgers used the Coliseum, they set virtually every attendance record possible. The season high of 2,253,887 was later broken in Dodger Stadium, but the single-game marks remain including the twi-night record of 72,140 against Cincinnati in 1961, which is still the major league record for an after-dark twin bill.

The reconstruction of the Coliseum led to one of those sensational baseball oddities. The left-field wall wasn't really a wall, but rather a huge screen forty-two feet high stretching from the corner into left center. The reason for this was the configuration of the Coliseum, which didn't really permit the comfortable installation of a baseball diamond. Thus a temporary installation was arranged which produced a left-field corner of 251 feet, shortest in the majors in this century. Left center, where the screen ended, was 320. In deepest center field a 6-foot fence was 420 feet from the plate, curving around to 380 in right center and 333 down the line in right. Behind the fence, it was another 119 feet to the seats in deepest center.

Duke Snider, famed for lofting the ball over the towering screen in Brooklyn, suddenly became a line drive hitter and his average went up. But it was Lee Walls, and then Wally Moon, who made the best work of the new layout. Moon, a left-hand hitter, perfected a stroke

The largest crowds in the history of major league baseball poured into the cavernous Los Angeles Coliseum, which was built for the 1932 Olympic Games. (*Photo courtesy of Los Angeles Dodgers*)

Major league baseball came to Los Angeles on this pitch thrown by Carl Erskine to the Giants' Jim Davenport. The opening day crowd in the Coliseum was 78,672, a big-league single-game record still unbroken. The center-field screen was about 190 feet from the permanent seats in the open end of the park. (*Photo courtesy of UPI*)

In addition to baseball, fans at Dodger Stadium have been treated to the antics of Casey Stengel (facing page). Stengel, a resident of nearby Glendale, is shown reenacting one of his famous gags. Rain is a rarity in Los Angeles, but Dodger Stadium was once flooded by pipe leakage. Here a local sportswriter (right) tests the water. (*Photos this page courtesy of Los Angeles Dodgers; photo facing page courtesy of UPI*)

Dodger Stadium was opened in 1962 and has since become the best attended park in the majors. In its first year, over 60 percent capacity attended games here, producing a season record attendance. (*Photo courtesy of Los Angeles Dodgers*)

that punched the ball high toward left, maddening pitchers and piling up extra base hits.

After finishing seventh in 1958, the Dodgers zoomed back to the top of the heap in 1959, winning a pennant playoff against Milwaukee and earning a berth in the World Series against the Chicago White Sox. That Series produced an attendance of 420,784, an all-time Series record despite being only six games. One of the games in Los Angeles also set the all-time single game record of 92,706.

In 1961 the expansion Angels came to L.A. and the Dodgers played their final season at the Coliseum. The pitchers, for the most part, were glad to get out of it in one piece.

Dodger Stadium, the last ballpark constructed with team capital, was opened in 1962. The Dodgers had their opening against Cincinnati on April 10 and lost 6–3. The Angels, as tenants, had theirs on April 17 and lost 5–3 to the Kansas City A's.

In its first season, Dodger Stadium provided a new single season attendance record. In its first five years of operation, it averaged over two million fans per year, matching a record of five straight two million seasons set by the postwar Yankees. In ten years, the total mounted to 21,484,861. Dodger owner Walter O'Malley demonstrated a point with his 56,000-seat ballpark. The capacity was small compared to the last two ballparks built from scratch before Dodger Stadium: Yankee Stadium (1923) and Cleveland Stadium (1932). Yet the very smallness of the park created a demand for tickets that resulted in a higher overall attendance in most seasons than had been achieved at the Coliseum, which was twice as large.

It was at Dodger Stadium that Sandy Koufax achieved many feats of pitching brilliance, including the perfect game against the helpless Cubs in 1965, his fourth no-hitter in as many seasons. It was the pitching combination of Koufax and Don Drysdale with the hitting of Tommy Davis that brought the Dodgers NL pennants in 1963, 1965, and 1966.

After 1965, when the Angels moved to Anaheim, the Dodgers had the park in Chavez Ravine all to themselves. But throughout the commotion attendant to record-shattering attendance, sensational pitching, and

World Series competition, Dodger Stadium retained its tranquil appearance. The lush grass and clean lines of the stadium give it something of the classic cut of the ballpark. Yet it has all modern necessities including the massive parking required for a West Coast ballpark, particularly a Southern California one.

In homage to the original ballpark, Dodger Stadium is located on Elysian Park Avenue. But it has gone the extra step suggested by William Cammeyer and built walls around the outfield. Behind those walls are bleacher sections in left field and right field. The bull pens are tucked in between the respective bleachers and the end of the main grandstand, which curves a few feet into fair territory. The park has unique ground-level boxes which give a dugout view of the game. But perhaps most unusual is the local habit of renting seat cushions at each game and then tossing them onto the field after the game is over.

Wrigley Field began as a minor league park in 1930 and ended as a city recreation area. In 1961 the Angels played here, giving both major leagues a club playing in ballparks with the same name that season. (*Photo courtesy of UPI*)

Milwaukee

Milwaukee has had a most unusual baseball history. Originally achieving major league status in 1878, the city has been unable to hold onto a permanent club in any big league despite setting attendance records. The first Milwaukee club was the National League team of 1878, which lasted only to the end of that season. In 1891 Milwaukee again returned to the majors with a one-season club in the American Association which closed up shop forever at the end of the season.

By virtue of holding one of the early franchises in the reorganized Western League, Milwaukee became a charter member of the American League in 1900. During its Western days, the Milwaukee club had been managed by Connie Mack. But in 1902 Ban Johnson shifted the Milwaukee team to St. Louis where it became the Browns, ultimately shifting again to Baltimore in 1954.

The original National League club played its games in a small wooden plant which seated about 3,000 and was also used briefly by the Western Association. Milwaukee really came to baseball prominence in the minor league American Association, which began functioning in 1902. The Brewer clubs in the new AA won eight pennants including those in the last two years of the their existence, 1951 and 1952.

A site for a new stadium was selected by local officials in 1909, but right until the end the Triple-A team was based in old Borchert Field. The final clearance for construction of a new park was given in 1950, and work was underway when the announcement came from Boston that the Braves were moving into Milwaukee for the 1953 season.

The AA club, managed by Rollie Hemsley, drew 195,839 fans at Borchert in 1952. Once the Braves determined to move to Milwaukee, the stadium concepts were revised. Another $500,000 was added to provide better seats, superior lighting, and other such items to raise the new stadium to major league standards. The total for construction rose to 5 million dollars. When President Lou Perini sold his former park, Braves Field in Boston, to Boston University it realized somewhere between $350,000 and $575,000, depending on how you figured it. However, Milwaukee's investment paid off handsomely. With its capacity increased to 35,911 for the Braves first season, the NL games drew a league record of 1,826,397 in 1953.

Milwaukee suddenly went bananas for baseball. Breweries, dairies, supermarkets, and utilities all joined in the mad rush to become associated with the Braves. Having drawn only 281,278 in their final Boston season, the Braves owners had reason to be pleased with themselves. Before the 1954 season opened, County Stadium's capacity was increased another 8,500 at a cost of $1,050,000. With a capacity of 44,091, the Braves pulled in 2,131,388 fans that season, breaking their own NL record for attendance. The entire state of Wisconsin joined in the madness. Players' pictures adorned billboards from one end of the state to the other, replica Braves' caps were the hottest selling item everywhere, and the *Milwaukee Sentinel*—the city's

morning paper—ran a front-page cartoon every day showing a Brave smiling, weeping, or ducking raindrops to indicate how the team did. On doubleheader days, the Brave cartoon sometimes had a split head.

During all of this hysteria, County Stadium had dimensions that showed 315 feet down the line in right, 402 feet to straightaway center, and 320 to the left-field corner. It had very much the appearance it has today after the expansion of 1954. County Stadium was not only the first ballpark built expressly for baseball with public funds, it was also the first ballpark ever to be built with light units attached. No park had been built since 1932—three years before night baseball came to the major leagues.

By 1957 the Braves had drawn two million or more fans for four straight seasons. That year they won their first pennant and broke the attendance record again, pulling 2,215,404 through the County Stadium turnstiles. After another pennant in 1958, things started going downhill. The Perini family sold the club, and the new owners didn't seem to hit it off with the Milwaukeeans. The team began to slide despite the presence in the lineup every day of such stars as Eddie Mathews and Hank Aaron. By the 1960s, attendance

Wintry weather is not uncommon in Milwaukee, but the excessive rain shown in the photo below is a bit unique. During the Braves' years here, Milwaukee frequently led the NL in attendance, but the AL Brewers have been unable to achieve those lofty figures thus far. (*Photo below courtesy of UPI; photo on preceding page courtesy of Milwaukee Brewers*)

was under one million; in 1965, it hit 555,584; and at the end of the season the Braves moved to Atlanta. The glee that had greeted their arrival thirteen seasons earlier was mirrored by the bitterness and anger that followed their departure. Lawsuits were filed against everybody in sight from the commissioner of baseball on down. The average fan, meanwhile, went back to enjoying the great Milwaukee beers and outstanding German food which are civic hallmarks.

After two years of silence, the prodigal son ventured a cautious return. The Chicago White Sox, struggling to make ends meet at Comiskey Park, scheduled a regular-season game against each AL club at County Stadium in 1968. Absent since 1901, the American League was back in Milwaukee. And something of a happy reunion it was, too. Baseball was alive in Milwaukee after all, the Sox averaging a staggering 29,494 baseball-starved fans per game there. When the AL expanded the next season, Milwaukee was peeved at being passed over in favor of Kansas City and, particularly, Seattle. But the White Sox added the two new clubs to their Milwaukee total, raising it to eleven games, and rumors abounded that the Sox would soon move northward.

Bud Selig, head of the local citizens' group actively seeking a new franchise for Milwaukee, was discouraged by his reaction from White Sox officials. But another 196,684 turned out for the eleven AL games in 1969. Then it happened. A chaotic situation in Seattle where poor attendance, a sub-par ballpark, and a horrid team combined to produce waves of financial red ink.

In 1970 the Seattle Pilots were to become the Milwaukee Brewers, and the charter members were back in the AL on their own again. The first year produced 933,690 paid fans, and although it dropped to 600,440 by 1972, the Brewer management persisted. With a con-

tending club in 1973, the gate soared over a million in Milwaukee for the first time since the Braves last did it in 1961.

The Brewers lean hard on their relationship with the community. In center field, "Bernie Brewer" dresses in a beer barrel and dances for joy when the home club does anything well. County Stadium also prides itself on having the "world's fastest infield sweep team" to smooth the infield dirt after five innings. They can turn the trick in less than a minute—but sometimes do appear to pay more attention to speed than smoothing the infield.

But, efficiency aside, the Brewer sweep crew is a good show. The energetic young men are costumed a la Bavarian beer-hall patrons, and they are accompanied by a girl with a broom who attends to the bases. "Bonnie Brewer" also engages in some byplay with the umpires and visiting coaches, such as kissing them and giving them a gentle swat with her broom. This type of activity originated in Baltimore in the late sixties with a young girl named Linda Wareheim. But the whole atmosphere in County Stadium imparts a distinctly Milwaukee flavor to the routine.

The National League heritage also remains in Milwaukee. AL crowds are historically more sedate and reserved than their NL counterparts. But during late-inning rallies by the home club at County Stadium, bedlam is the order of the day on every pitch. Unlike many teams that try to evoke such response artificially, the Brewers normally let the crowd do the work. As visiting players will attest, they do it well. One AL traveling secretary remarked after his team blew three straight in County Stadium, "Those crowds are like the National League."

Minnesota

Up in Minnesota, baseball used to be a part-time diversion for those who weren't going fishing that particular day. It may still be that way in the summer, but since 1961 the proportions have shifted somewhat in favor of baseball. That was the year that the major leagues came to the north woods, the Washington Senators moving their American League franchise to Minnesota.

Actually, the movement that brought big-league baseball to Minnesota began in 1954 when the first work was done by the construction firm of Johnson, Drake, and Piper on what would eventually become Metropolitan Stadium. Located at 80th Street and Cedar Avenue in suburban Bloomington, Metropolitan Stadium is designed to serve the twin Minnesota cities of Minneapolis and St. Paul. But when it was first ready for play in 1956, it was the Minneapolis Millers of the American Association who moved from their old Nicollet Park into the New Met. The St. Paul Saints, the sister AA team of the Millers, remained in their Lexington Park in St. Paul.

Both triple-A clubs disappeared in 1961 when the Minnesota Twins were born of the transfer by Calvin Griffith of the original Senators from Washington. The Met was unusual in that it was designed for expansion, and expanded it was when the Twins became the prime tenants. During the days when the Millers played minor league ball there, the Met had a capacity of 21,688. Its present capacity, after several expansions, is 45,919 for baseball.

Owing to its novel concept as an expandable ball-park, the Met today still has a somewhat skeletal look about it, poking up like a giant erector set from its pleasant but barren surroundings. From the third deck behind home plate the view presented is one of cows grazing contentedly in faraway fields. Up close is the all-too-familiar specter of automobiles huddled together around the outer rim of the park as if drawn mothlike to its light.

Cold can be a problem in the Met, and so can the stiff winds which occasionally gust outbound at a rate of fifty miles per hour or more. Hitters generally respond with more enthusiasm to this situation than pitchers, who watch helplessly as their best efforts go darting into the bleachers in the cozy power alleys, 365 feet away or less. The publicity department of the Twins has a master chart that lists each seat and position beyond the fences. When a homerun is hit in the Met, and they come in bunches, the number of feet it traveled is announced precisely.

To encourage long-ball hitting, the power alleys have been periodically readjusted. For 1975 the left-center alley was drawn in to 350 feet while the right-center alley remained at 373 feet. It is 330 feet down each line and 410 to straightaway center field. From its first season, the Met developed a well-deserved reputation as a homer-hitter haven and the management just tries to help things along a little. During the early 1970s the trend was to stretch the park out a bit, since the visiting teams were hitting more homers than the Twins. Minnesota had moved away from the slugging style of the original club (Harmon Killebrew, Bob Allison, Jim

(*Photo below courtesy of UPI; photo on pages 130–131 courtesy of Minnesota Twins*)

Lemon, et al.) to more of a line drive style of hitting a la Tony Oliva and Rod Carew. For instance, in 1971, 128 homers were hit in the Met, but only 57 by the Twins (Killebrew had 15 of those). The following year, 106 were hit in a slightly larger park.

From the fans' point of view, the weather is not much of a factor. Minnesotans are more than used to the cold weather and chilling winds. They come prepared. Early season and late season games have been sparsely attended in recent years not because of the weather, but because the Twins have not had a contending club. In years past, reasonably large crowds would appear attired for the occasion in parkas, ski jackets, and blankets in a riot of color.

As might be suspected, no-hitters have been as scarce as championships around the Met. In fact, there has been one of each. Jack Kralick got the no-hitter in 1962, the second season in the park, when he beat Kansas City 1–0 on August 26. The championship came in 1965 when the Twins came home in front of the pack in the American League and faced the Dodgers in the World Series. Some of the best pitching the Twins had the misfortune to be exposed to came during that series when Sandy Koufax, pitching despite arm miseries, threw a pair of complete games in which he allowed no runs and only seven hits total in the two games. His first start in game two, however, resulted in his being removed under fire. The Twins knocked out Don Drysdale in a wild six-run third inning and won the first World Series game ever played in Minnesota, 8–2.

The next day Minnesota took a two-games-to-none lead in the series with a 5–1 win. Then the scene shifted to Los Angeles, where the Dodgers swept three games. With their backs to the wall, the Twins came through with a clutch 5–0 victory in the sixth game at Minnesota. Jim (Mudcat) Grant cooled off the blazing Dodger bats with a six-hitter. Grant helped his own cause with a three-run homer, and Allison slammed a two-run shot to account for the other Twin runs.

The seventh game at Minnesota turned out to be another celebration of the mound artistry of Koufax. Almost untouchable from the start, Sandy spun a sparkling three-hit shutout to win 2–0. The Dodgers scored twice in the fourth of Jim Kaat when journeyman outfielder Lou Johnson cracked a homer, Ron Fairly doubled, and Wes Parker singled him home.

After the championship season the Twins remained prime contenders, finishing second the next two years. In 1969 and 1970 the club won the West Division title only to be eliminated by the Baltimore Orioles in straight games each year in the divisional playoffs. Since then it has been downhill at the Met. The attendance, which hadn't gone under a million during the first ten years in Minnesota, dropped to 940,858 in 1971 and was 797,901 in 1972. The Twins showed some improvement in 1973, but only a consistent contender is likely to pull the Minnesotans away from their wide variety of outdoor diversions in the upper Midwest and cause them to put down that fishing pole long enough to drive to Bloomington for games at the Met.

Montreal

Baseball goes bilingual at Jarry Park. A night with the Expos is as colorful as an evening on the town in Montreal itself.

Fans arrive early to watch the *lanceurs* (pitchers) warm up, having purchased their *billets* (tickets) and gotten comfortable in the *loges* (boxes), *estrade* (grandstand), or *estrade populaire* (bleachers) where they may have *sièges reserves* (reserved seats).

But baseball is baseball in any language and, for their part, the largely French-speaking population of Montreal has embraced the game with a passion previously reserved for hockey. The city of Montreal proper has a population of 1,214,300. Jarry Park has a capacity of 28,000. During its first five years in the National League (1969 to 1973) the Expos attracted 6,317,262 paying fans, an average of 1,263,452 per season. This means that on any night of the season two out of every three seats in the tiny ballpark are occupied.

The proximity of the fans to the action at Jarry Park is one of the things that makes baseball in Montreal so appealing. The park is actually a temporary structure that was built in 1969 to provide a home for the Expos until a permanent stadium could be constructed. Present plans call for the team to move into the huge new stadium being built for the 1976 Olympic Games. In the meantime, Montreal fans have the opportunity to enjoy conditions that no longer prevail in most parks south of the United States border.

The fact that Jarry Park exists at all is a tribute to Montreal's dynamic mayor, Jean Drapeau. When the National League awarded Montreal the first franchise ever issued outside of the United States, Drapeau energetically pursued the construction of a home for the team and the work, started during the winter of 1968 to 1969, was far enough advanced for opening day to be held on schedule.

Probably the first big shock to the NL owners was the overflow crowd that poured into the tiny park on April 14, 1969, for Canada's first major league baseball game. Montreal fans turned out in force, exceeding the listed capacity by more than a thousand and the actual capacity by probably more than that since the park was still in the early stages of completion. The second shock came when the Expos left their new fans limp with a wild 8–7 victory over the defending league champion St. Louis Cardinals.

Whatever the impression left from that exciting opener, it must have been lasting. Although the Expos have never had a club finish higher than fourth in their six-team division, attendance has been constantly strong. The smallish size of Jarry Park tends to serve as an asset for the club. Knowing the shortage of seats, fans tend to buy well in advance for the games. This prevents the fans from waiting to determine the quality of the weather on game day before they come out and buy tickets. Fans with tickets already purchased and money thereby invested are more likely to come regardless of the weather than undecided fans awaiting sunshine. Montreal thus produces a very hardy breed of fan who patiently sits through wind, cold, rain, and sometimes snow for his baseball.

It will be interesting to observe the net effect on Expo

attendance when they eventually leave Jarry Park for a larger, probably domed, stadium.

At present, Jarry Park is an equitable place for both hitters and pitchers. In its early days it had a reputation as a homerun park. This, however, was evidently due in the main to the inconsistency of Expo pitching. As the team has improved, the number of homers has tended to decline. In 1970, 168 round-trippers sailed out of Jarry. The next season, the total was 153, which placed Jarry Park second only to Atlanta as a homer haven. But only 50 of these were hit by the Expos. In 1972 the Expos again hit 50, but the total of homers dropped to 106 overall in the park. Now, with the development of Ken Singleton as a legitimate power hitter, the total has started to rise but only in proportion to an increase of homers by the Expos.

Since its opening, Jarry Park has been enclosed by a wire fence which is 340 feet down the right-field line, 420 to dead center, and 340 to left. The power alleys are a comfortable 368 feet from the plate. Balls hit over the wall in right, where there are no seats, will often carry into the public swimming pool outside the park if they don't hit the *tableau indicateur* (scoreboard).

Jarry Park has a single deck on three sides with seats extending to the corner in right and the corner in left. In left field there is an open bleacher that has reserved seats in its front portion and unreserved seats in its back areas. Except for the boxes, most of the seats in the park are backless, bleacher-style continuous rows.

Jarry Park has an unusual atmosphere—in part be-

cause of its location. Though it is in a major city, it is suburban and is also located in the midst of what was a small public park. It isn't quite Parisian, but almost. The bilingual condition produces everything in duplicate: public address announcements, radio broadcasts, scorecard comments, signs, and advertisements. The French language produces reasonable equivalents of common baseball terminology like *lanceurs* (pitchers), *receveurs* (catchers), *interieurs* (infielders), and *voltigeurs* (outfielders). Some things have to be taken a bit more literally. For instance runs are *points*, but hits are *coups surs* and errors are, alas, still *erreurs*.

By virtue of being Canada's only major league baseball team, the Expos tend to draw from a range of population far outside of the normal zone. Many fans from across the border regularly attend games at Jarry Park, and Expo games are broadcast on radio stations in Vermont and upstate New York. Other fans come from the predominantly French parts of Quebec province and still others from English Canada to the west (Ottawa, Toronto, Hamilton) with regularity. Expo games are also broadcast as far east as St. John, New Brunswick, and as far west as Toronto. The Canadian Broadcasting System's national television network carries many Expo games across the nation, thus making the Expos an all-Canada interest.

All of this press interest springs from the only covered part of Jarry Park, the *galerie de la presse* (press box).

New York

Baseball may well have had its beginning as an organized game in New York. Alexander Cartwright's claim to be the man who invented the standard version of the game is both reasonable and strong. But regardless of the claims of paternity, baseball—in its now familiar form—very early became an intensely popular game in New York. Much of the game's early history revolves around New York, and its teams won the first two recognized national championships.

In 1845 Cartwright's Knickerbockers began the practice of playing competitive games. However, since they had just lately been ejected from their former home on 26th Street and Madison Avenue, they moved their games to Elysian Fields in Hoboken, New Jersey, across the Hudson River. There, on June 19, 1846, they played the New York Nine. The New York club beat the Knickerbockers, 23–1, in a four-inning game. For the next three years the Knickerbockers devoted themselves to intraclub games. In 1849 they adopted the blue and white uniform in the high-collar, long-pants style that they were to make popular and became the first uniformly outfitted team.

The activities of the Knickerbockers, though Cartwright had left the club and traveled west (eventually settling in Hawaii), attracted substantial attention among the young men of New York, and they soon began to form baseball clubs in imitation. By the 1850s there were several such clubs in New York, and in 1852 the first Brooklyn teams were organized. In 1858 all-star clubs from the two cities met in a three-game series for the national championship at the former National Race Course, then known as the Fashion Race Course, on Long Island in what is now the borough of Queens.

New York won that series in 1858 and again in 1859. Brooklyn got its first National title in 1861 and Brooklyn clubs won the next four championships. The Unions of New York won in 1868, and the Atlantics of Brooklyn collected another crown in 1870. To say that New York and Brooklyn teams dominated baseball in the amateur era would be something of an understatement; between the two cities a total of nine championships were won in thirteen years of formal competition.

Thanks to William Cammeyer, Brooklyn stole the march on New York when it came to ballpark development. When league play was inaugurated in 1871, the Mutuals represented New York, but they played at Cammeyer's Union Grounds in Brooklyn. Frankly, Brooklyn would not have been anxious to claim them as its own. The Mutuals went through five managers in as many years, including Cammeyer himself in 1873, with four second-division finishes the result. A second place in 1874 was the best finish in the five years of the National Association and that season the Mutuals were seven and a half games behind Boston. In 1876 Cammeyer took the reigns again for the first NL season and produced a sixth place in the standings. After the Mutuals were expelled from the National League at the end of that season, New York was without a club in the major leagues until 1883.

Then they came back with a vengeance. Two clubs, the Mets in the American Association and the Giants in the National League, appeared in 1883, both owned by

Initially home for publisher James Gordon Bennett's polo clubs, the original Polo Grounds turned to baseball in 1880. The nonleague Mets were the first club, but the Giants brought baseball fame to the Fifth Avenue site before it was torn down in 1888. (*Photo courtesy of Harry M. Stevens & Co.*)

John Day. The next season, the AA club won its pennant but lost the postseason World Series in straight games. Then Day, disgusted with the Mets' loss, "traded" two of their star players to the Giants, thus virtually ruining the AA team. Scandalized by the deal, the league tried to expel the Mets but failed and eventually the team shipped out to Staten Island.

While the NL remained snugly in the Polo Grounds, the AA team, called the New York Metropolitans (or Mets for short), were sold to Erastus Wiman. Wiman owned transit and entertainment facilities on Staten Island and saw the ballclub as a valuable traffic-builder for his other enterprises. He built a new park for the club and spent lavishly to advertise them. Of all the New York ballparks, the St. George Grounds left the most interesting footnote in history. The Mets were a virtual disaster from the day they arrived at St. George until 1887 when they finally left the AA. Wiman had, however, built a decent park adjacent to the site of the

cricket grounds upon which Miss Mary Outerbridge had supposedly introduced the game of tennis to the United States.

In 1889 when the Giants were dispossessed from the original Polo Grounds, they too found their way to Staten Island and the St. George Grounds. For twenty-five games the Giants held forth on Staten Island. They were aided somewhat in their performance by the fact that the outfield was frequently flooded and covered with board to give it some footing. The Giants were familiar with this terrain and the visiting teams obviously were not. In all, the Giants drew 57,260 fans to Staten Island for their games, and the Giant president initially announced he might make the park the permanent home for the club. But as soon as a new Manhattan park became available, the Giants left and the career of Staten Island as a major league site was ended.

The Giants had New York all to themselves until 1903, when Ban Johnson moved the Baltimore club in his upstart American League into Manhattan as part of the price of peace between the two major leagues.

Johnson's intentions had previously roused Giant owner Andrew Freedman into action. Freedman, hardly one of New York's more genteel men, was well connected politically and sought to use that influence to preclude AL rivalry with his club in Manhattan. Freedman's strategy was a marvel of simplicity. By using his political clout to run a street through the middle of any potential site for an AL ballpark, he felt he could effectively prevent Johnson from placing a team in the city.

Johnson, not to be easily foiled, sought owners who could negate Freedman where it counted—City Hall. The AL president found his men in Frank Farrell and Bill Devery. Farrell ran a gambling operation near the Astor Hotel which was frequented by the city's social and political elite. Devery was cited by the New York press as the most corrupt policeman in city history. They were more than a match for Freedman, who shortly sold the Giants.

Farrell and Devery picked coal merchant Joseph Gordon as their front man, and while Gordon served as president of the club his two cohorts grabbed a piece of land on Broadway between 165th and 168th Streets. In three months they slapped together a ballpark which seated about 15,000.

Hilltop Park, as it was commonly known, was formally entitled the New York American League Ball-

After the fire of April 1911, a fourth Polo Grounds was built, this one of concrete and steel. Surveying the work in August was the trio of Harry M. Stevens, founder of the famous concession company; builder John Foster; and Giants president John T. Brush. The new building literally cemented the unique configuration of the Polo Grounds forever. (*Photos courtesy of Harry M. Stevens & Co.*)

park, and the paint was still wet when the Yankees made their debut on April 30, 1903, before an overflow audience of 16,293. The Yankees, nicknamed the Highlanders in those early days, beat Washington 6–2. But the field was hardly in an advanced state of readiness. It was uneven and rocky, making fielding something more of a hazard than usual.

The Yankees survived their first season at the Hilltop and, in fact, drew 211,808 into the cozy little wooden grandstands. They may have been drawn in part by the view afforded from the upper rows of the stands, which gave a clear look at the Hudson River and the New Jersey Palisades.

In 1904 the Yankees drew people to watch baseball. They stayed in the pennant race to the final day of the season and closed the campaign with a doubleheader against first place Boston at the Hilltop. Jack Chesbro won an AL record forty-one games for the Yanks that year but earned goat horns when he wild-pitched Boston's Lou Criger home from third with the decisive run in the first game, giving Boston the pennant.

A fire that destroyed the Polo Grounds grandstand brought the Giants into the Hilltop in 1911. They played their first NL game there on April 15, defeating the Dodgers 6–3. The Giants returned to the new Polo Grounds in June, but their visit was to have further consequences when Giant president John T. Brush invited the Yankees to share his park starting in 1913.

Hilltop Park was entirely wooden with a single-deck covered grandstand extending between first and third

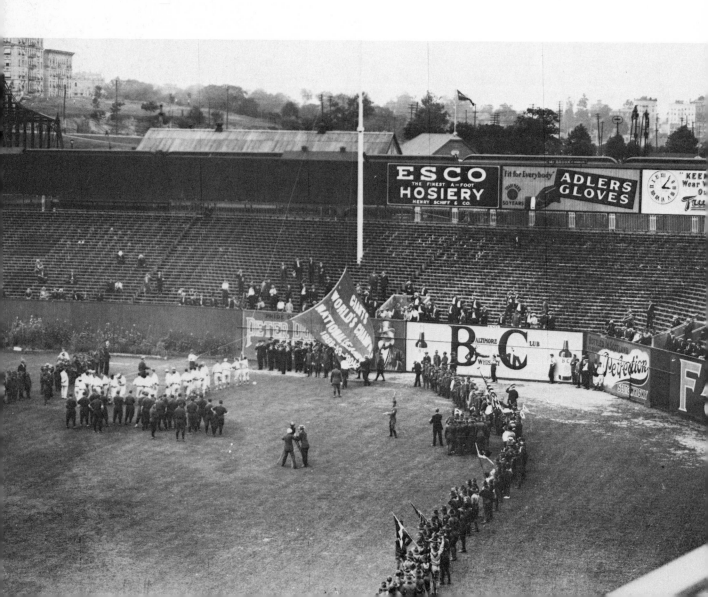

Even after the fire destroyed the main wooden grandstand, wooden bleachers (bottom left) remained in the Polo Grounds at 157th Street. In 1913 the Yankees moved in as tenants. Here their manager Frank Chance shakes hands with old pal Ira Thomas of Philadelphia. (*Photos pages 140–144 courtesy of UPI*)

bases, open board-type bleachers extending to the right-field corner, and a partly covered stand going down the left-field line into the corner. The scoreboard was located in left near the foul line. There was a large exit gate for the bleacherites in right-field fair territory.

The finale for this quaint little park was a bizarre one. *The New York Times'* writer on the scene said, "No such travesty on the national game has ever before been staged on the Hilltop and it is doubtful if any major league ground has seen its equal." The irrepressible clowns from Washington were responsible for this admonishment. On October 5, 1912, Washington came to Hilltop Park with a shot at second place. The Senators, managed by former Yankee Clark Griffith, took a 5–1 lead after their turn at bat in the fourth. But Griffith then learned that Boston had beaten Philadelphia and second place was no longer at issue. He then elected to turn loose his cast of diamond characters. Washington became more interested in clowning and entertaining the crowd of some 5,000 than winning, thus squandering its lead. Nick Altrock and Germany Schaefer led the clowning and each took turns pitching and playing other positions after starter Tom Hughes

departed in the fifth. The Yankees finally won the game 8–6 when Hal Chase smacked a homer over the wall in right with two men on, ending ten years of baseball history at Hilltop Park. The Dodgers, meanwhile, played their final game at Washington Park on the same day in Brooklyn, thus ending the chapters of the last two wooden ballparks in New York.

Polo Grounds

The first professional league grounds in New York proper were opened on September 29, 1880, when the Metropolitans took the field against the National club of Washington at the Polo Grounds. The Mets proved that New York was a fertile baseball market and played 151 games in 1881. John B. Day moved into the big time in a big way in 1883 when he entered the Mets in the

American Association and bought the Troy, New York, franchise in the National League and moved it to New York City.

Day set up both of his teams at the Polo Grounds, between Fifth and Sixth avenues bounded by 110th and 112th streets, which he had converted for baseball. The first NL game ever played in New York took place at the Polo Grounds on Tuesday, May 1, when the Giants faced Boston in a game that began at 4:00 P.M. and included former president U. S. Grant among the audience. Grant, it was reliably reported, sat in the rear of the main stand and joined several times in "the applause accorded the players." At 3:25, the first gong sounded for Boston to take the field for a fifteen-minute drill. At 3:40, the second gong sounded for New York to do likewise. Then captains Buck Ewing of New York and Jack Burdock of Boston tossed for innings, Burdock winning. Boston elected to send New York to bat first, reserving last bats for themselves. The largest crowd in New York baseball history up to that time (estimated at 15,000) was entertained by Grafulia's 7th Regiment Band.

When the game got under way, Ewing struck out as the first batter, but New York scored three runs. Roger Connor's triple off the right-field wall was the big hit, and the Giants hung on to win 7–5.

The next day the Giants also won the second game of the series, 3–2. Before the week was out, Day had returned to the old practice of allowing the grounds to be used by other clubs. The Stock Exchange team defeated college clubs from Rose Hill and Manhattan on May 9 and 10. Then, on May 12, the first AA game in New York history was played, the Mets facing the Philadelphia Athletics. Oddly, the Philadelphia pitcher was Bobby Mathews, a former Mutual. He was opposed by Tim Keefe of the Mets. The Athletics were too much for manager Jim Mutrie's men that day and won 11–4.

The following season, however, the Mets were the class of the AA and won New York's first pennant. They earned the right to face the Providence Grays in the first fully sanctioned World Series. Providence was a one-man gang, and that man was Charlie (Old Hoss) Radbourn who had pitched seventy-two games during the season and won sixty of them. He added three more to his string in the Series. The Series began at the Polo Grounds on October 23, 1884, and a crowd of eighteen hundred saw Radbourn two-hit the Mets and Keefe, 6–0. The following day, Radbourn again bested

Keefe, 3–1, and the attendance shrank to one thousand. On October 25 Radbourn finished it off, 12–2, with Jim (Buck) Becannon taking the loss as Keefe switched to umpiring. Mercifully, umpire Keefe called the game after six innings due to supposed "darkness," and the first official World Series was over.

So, too, was the role of the Mets as a building power in New York baseball. Day had always hoped that the Giants would do better than the Mets because the NL charged fifty cents per ticket for its games and the AA only twenty-five.

Day stripped the Mets of their manager and leading stars after the 1884 Series fiasco. This enraged the AA directors. Day deliberately set about destroying the Mets by giving them the worst choice of dates at the Polo Grounds and even played them in the morning when the Giants were home in the preferred afternoon times. At the insistence of the AA, Day sold the Mets to Wiman after the 1885 season, and they languished on Staten Island for two years before disbanding.

In February 1889 the Giants were reigning baseball champions. They had won their first pennant in 1888 and defeated St. Louis, the AA champs, six games to four, in the postseason Series. But at that point, Day got the shocking news that the city was going to tear down the Polo Grounds grandstand to complete what is now Douglass Circle at 110th Street and Fifth Avenue. The Giants offered to donate $10,000 to charity for another year in the park. The usual route of tying matters up in the courts through bribery had failed. The city's leading sporting paper, the *New York Clipper*, said, "The Polo Grounds seems almost like part of the club, and to deprive the club of its grounds is like depriving it of part of its honor." Honor, charity, courts, bribery, and all notwithstanding, the Polo Grounds was going and the world champion baseball team was without a home. Day took the club to Jersey City's Oakland Park for the first two home games of the season and then to St. George Grounds for twenty-five more.

But, in the meantime, the state legislature passed a bill allowing the use of Manhattan Field, uptown at 155th Street and Eighth Avenue, as a baseball park.

Day, of course, was behind this move and made the most of it. By June, construction on a new park was well under way. Fences were already up, and five hundred men were working on the building. On July 8, 1889, the Giants beat Pittsburgh, 7–5, and inaugurated the new Polo Grounds. The grandstand, though not as

If Brooklyn's Ebbets Field was dominated by its colorful sights and carnivallike atmosphere, the Polo Grounds was dominated by its shape. Often described as horseshoelike, it was really more bathtublike. The incredibly close corners in left and right made every batter potentially dangerous. Pitchers sought to induce hitters to hit into straightaway center, where 400-foot drives were playable. (*Photo courtesy of UPI*)

(OVERLEAF)
The Harlem River flows placidly between the opposing camps in New York's basel war—the Polo Grounds on the left bank, Yankee Stadium on the right. The Polo Grou was expanded in 1924 after the Yankees opened their huge stadium following their e tion from the Polo Grounds by the Giants. (*Photo courtesy of UPI; photo page 151 co tesy of Wide World*)

laborate as the ones in Philadelphia and Boston, was large. It extended 410 feet along 155th Street and 320 feet along the third base line beneath Coogan's Bluff. The stands were in the shape of a large segment of a circle with straight sides. The lower tier was fifty feet deep and the upper deck thirty-one feet deep. The grandstand held 5,500 and additional bleachers raised the capacity to 15,000. The entire affair was built with frame trusses bolted together. The Giants repeated as NL champions that year and dispatched Brooklyn, the AA titlists, six games to three in the Series.

The Players League war of 1890 created one of the most peculiar situations in baseball history in New York. The Brotherhood of Professional Base Ball Players was a union to which virtually all players in the major leagues, the NL and AA, belonged. When a series of labor-management confrontations finally came to a head in 1889, the players decided to go forward on their own and form a league which they would run. This was, in effect, a throwback to the previously unsuccessful National Association, also a player-run organization.

Colonel E. A. McAlpin and Edward B. Talcott, the backers of the New York club in the Players League, built a large grandstand for their club on a piece of land immediately north of Day's Polo Grounds. Often the two clubs were home on the same day and games took place simultaneously at both the 155th Street and 157th Street ends of the block.

On May 12, 1890, Mike Tiernan of the Giants achieved a unique feat in baseball history. Tiernan slugged a long homer over the center-field fence of the Polo Grounds. The ball sailed into the outside fence of Brotherhood Park next door, and as Tiernan toured the bases he was cheered by fans from both parks.

When the PL war ended, the Brotherhood club folded and Day purchased the larger park, moving the Giants a few hundred feet north and renaming the structure the New Polo Grounds. The Giants took permanent possession on April 22, 1891, before the largest opening-day New York baseball crowd ever at the time, 17,335, but lost to Boston 4–3.

John McGraw became the Giant manager in 1902 and led the club to pennants in 1904 and 1905. The Giants were to embark on other pennant years in 1911, 1912, and 1913. But they suffered a slight detour after the second game of the 1911 season. The Polo Grounds was destroyed by fire. After the first two games of the season had been played, a fire broke out on Friday morn-

ing, April 14. It consumed the entire main stand, leaving only about 10,000 wooden bleachers undamaged.

Giant president John Brush bypassed competitive bidding and immediately started work rebuilding the Polo Grounds as a concrete and steel building. At the invitation of Yankee president Frank Farrell, the Giants played at Hilltop Park in the interim. The new stands opened on June 28, 1911, with 16,000 seats ready for the public. But only 6,000 showed up for the first game. Work continued until the World Series that fall by which time 34,000 seats were available, including the 10,000 in the wooden bleachers in left and right fields.

A formal dedication was held the following spring. The new stands were built in the same configuration and location as the old wooden ones, facing east toward the Harlem River and Eighth Avenue with its back to Coogan's Bluff. The two decks were faced with a decorative frieze on the facade. This frieze, which was to disappear when the park was renovated some years later, contained a series of allegorical treatments in bas relief. Pylons in neo-Roman style flanked the horseshoe stand. The box seats were in the style of the royal boxes of the Colosseum in Rome. In 1924 the ballpark was reconstructed with the second deck extended into the outfield on both sides, leaving only the small bleacher in center uncovered. The capacity was increased from 34,000 to 55,000.

Under McGraw, the Giants won pennants in 1921, 1922, 1923, and 1924. After his retirement, Bill Terry led the club to more flags in 1933, 1936, and 1937. But the most famous single moment in Polo Grounds history was to come in 1951.

On Wednesday, October 3, 34,320 fans were on hand to watch the third and deciding game of the NL playoffs between the Giants and Dodgers. Brooklyn went to the home ninth leading 4–1. The Giants scored a run off Don Newcombe and had two men on when Ralph Branca came in to face Bobby Thomson. Thomson hit the second pitch into the lower left deck for a three-run homer, a 5–4 victory, and a pennant. Leo Durocher, the 1951 manager, also managed the Giants in 1954 when they won their last New York pennant and stunned Cleveland in four straight games in the World Series, largely on the heroics of pinch-hitting Dusty Rhodes.

After the renovation of 1924, the next major change to come at the Polo Grounds was in 1940, when lights were installed and the first night game was played on

May 24 against the Boston Braves. Despite winning thirteen pennants up to that time, the Giants had never drawn a million fans in a season at the Polo Grounds. They broke that barrier for the first time in 1945 and set their all-time New York record of 1,600,793 in 1947 with a fourth-place club managed by Mel Ott. The team that year included some fearsome sluggers: Walker Cooper, Johnny Mize, Willard Marshall, Sid Gordon, and a rookie named Bobby Thomson. Mize tied for the NL lead in homers with 51 and the team set a league record of 221.

When the Giants moved to San Francisco after the 1957 season, the Polo Grounds became the scene for soccer, basketball, midget auto racing, boxing, and other attractions. In 1960 pro football returned with the American Football League and its New York Titans. But in 1962 the Polo Grounds once again rang out with the sounds of baseball. The New York Mets, a hapless expansion club in the NL, occupied the ballpark for two seasons while the new Shea Stadium was being built.

As was fitting for the early Mets of Casey Stengel, they lost the first game they ever played in the historic Polo Grounds, 4–3, to Pittsburgh on April 13, 1962, on a ninth-inning wild pitch. They were also beaten, 5–1 by Philadelphia, in the final NL game ever played there on September 18, 1964. Following the Mets departure to Shea Stadium, the one-time home of Mc-Graw, Ott, and Willie Mays was demolished and became additional acreage for a housing development that already adjoined it to the north.

Yankee Stadium

Without doubt, the New York Yankees rate as baseball's most successful nomadic tribe.

During the seventy-odd seasons since their inception, the Yankees have built and occupied the most magnificent structure ever constructed expressly for baseball, served twice as tenants of two different New York National League clubs, and struggled along during their first ten years in a jerry-built wooden ballpark.

From Hilltop Park, where they played from 1903 to 1912, the Yankees moved into the Polo Grounds. They played their games in the Giants' park when they were purchased by the two colonels who were to change their destiny, T. L. Huston and Jacob Ruppert. By 1920, the first season after Babe Ruth's purchase from Boston, the Yankees were outdrawing the Giants in the Polo Grounds and were no longer welcome as tenants. The 1920 Yankee attendance of 1,289,422 was a major league record at the time.

After being told by the Giants to find a new home, Ruppert bought the land of a former lumberyard in the Bronx immediately across the Harlem River from the Polo Grounds and set about to build the greatest baseball stadium in the sport's history. He succeeded.

The opening of Yankee Stadium on April 18, 1923, was one of the two or three most sensational opening days in baseball annals. Though the huge triple-tiered main stands extended only from slightly past first base to slightly past third base at the time, the stadium was considered a magnificent edifice in its day and, in fact, for decades afterward. The results of the first game magnified its awesome presence. The Yankees beat Boston 4–1 when Babe Ruth smashed a long three-run homer for the decisive runs. The crowd was announced by Edward Barrow, the Yankee general manager, as 74,217, though that figure was reduced over the year to a more realistic figure. Whatever the number, the crowd was huge by 1920s baseball standards. It was huge by any standards. It packed into the main stand, jammed into the huge wooden bleacher which completely encircled the remainder of the plot between 157th and 161st streets on River Avenue, and spilled over into the street where thousands were turned away.

The Yankees rolled to their third AL championship that season and beat the Giants in the World Series for their first world title in the fall. They captured flags in 1926, 1927, 1928, and 1932 before the end of the Ruth era. The pennant parade continued with Lou Gehrig and Joe DiMaggio in 1936, 1937, 1938, and 1939 as the Yankees became the first AL club to win four straight titles and the first team in baseball to take the World Series in four successive years.

After Gehrig's tragic death, the Yankees continued to tower over baseball with pennants in 1941, 1942, 1943, 1947, 1949, 1950, and 1951 before DiMaggio retired, winning the Series every year except 1942. Yogi Berra and Mickey Mantle led the Yankees to more titles in 1952, 1953, 1955, 1956, 1957, 1958, 1960, 1961, 1962, 1963, and 1964—in the process making the Bronx

(*Yearbook and newspaper clippings from Shannon Collection*)

Bombers the first club ever to win *five* straight pennants *and* World Series (1949–1953).

For a fan, baseball knew few moments as impressive as an Old Timers' Day at Yankee Stadium when the twenty-nine pennants and twenty World Championship banners were hung from the facade of the third deck. It was a truly tingling sports moment.

Colonel Ruppert and his trusty aide-de-camp Ed Barrow were always opposed to the installation of lights, feeling it both beneath the dignity of baseball's most powerful club and detrimental to the appearance of their massive stadium. When the triumvirate of Larry MacPhail, Dan Topping, and Del Webb took over the Yankees, one of their first moves was to put in lights. On May 28, 1946, the first night game was played at Yankee Stadium. Perhaps unused to the lights, the Yankees lost to Washington, 2–1.

Night baseball and the postwar boom in sports produced the largest attendance figures in Yankee Stadium's history. During the five years from 1946 to 1950, Yankee games at the stadium drew over two million each season, a total of 11,181,406 in five years, and a record 2,373,901 in 1948, although the team didn't win the pennant. The Yanks were the first team ever to draw over two million for five straight years, a record since matched by the Los Angeles Dodgers; and the single-season mark has subsequently been eclipsed by both Cleveland and Los Angeles. But the Yankees were operating in a hotly competitive three-club market. In 1947 the Giants, Yankees, and Dodgers combined for an attendance of 5,587,256 among them.

Yankee Stadium did not spring forth whole. It was gradually completed with sections of the wooden bleacher removed and the main concrete and steel stand

extended into right and left fields. The first such change came in 1928 when the left-field stands were completed. Right field was extended in 1937, concluding the ellipse with its large open bleachers in the center-field area. Such structure changes also altered the playing field dimensions.

Originally, Yankee Stadium was 490 feet to center, 295 down the line in right, and 281 into the left corner. The completion of construction left the right-field corner almost unchanged but extended the left-field line by 20 feet and drew center field in slightly.

The gradual changing of the structure also had the effect of reducing the seating capacity, which was once advertised at 80,000. The exchange of wooden bleachers for chair-type seats with arms gave each fan a bit more room, eliminated the potential for continuous selling by making more reserved seats, and reduced the overall total that could be accommodated. After the completion of the concrete bleacher, Yankee Stadium held 67,163. Further renovations during the years of ownership by the Columbia Broadcasting System reduced it further to 65,010.

Among the many notable exploits in Yankee Stadium were Babe Ruth's sixtieth homerun in 1927, Don Larsen's perfect-game no-hitter in the 1956 World Series, and Roger Maris's sixty-first homerun in 1961. But it

Hilltop Park was built by political interests as the home of the AL club, then called the Highlanders because of the elevation of the park above its surroundings. Columbia Presbyterian Medical Center now occupies the principal portion of the site. Several colleges also played here during the early 1900s. (*Photo courtesy of New York Yankees*)

When Jake Ruppert went out looking for a ballpark site, he found an old lumberyard on the east bank of the Harlem River. In a year, with the help of a few million brewery dollars, he turned the old lumberyard into Yankee Stadium. (*Photos courtesy of New York Yankees*)

(*Photos courtesy of UPI*)

(*Photo courtesy of UPI*)

(*Photo above and photo right courtesy of UPI*)

(Scorecard from Shannon Collection)

Fans go onto the field at Yankee Stadium after the final home game of the 1973 season. A remodeled Yankee Stadium is scheduled to open in 1976, but it will be without the characteristic facade and many other famous physical features of the celebrated "House that Ruth Built." (*Photos here, top of page 158, and pages 162–163 by George Kalinsky*)

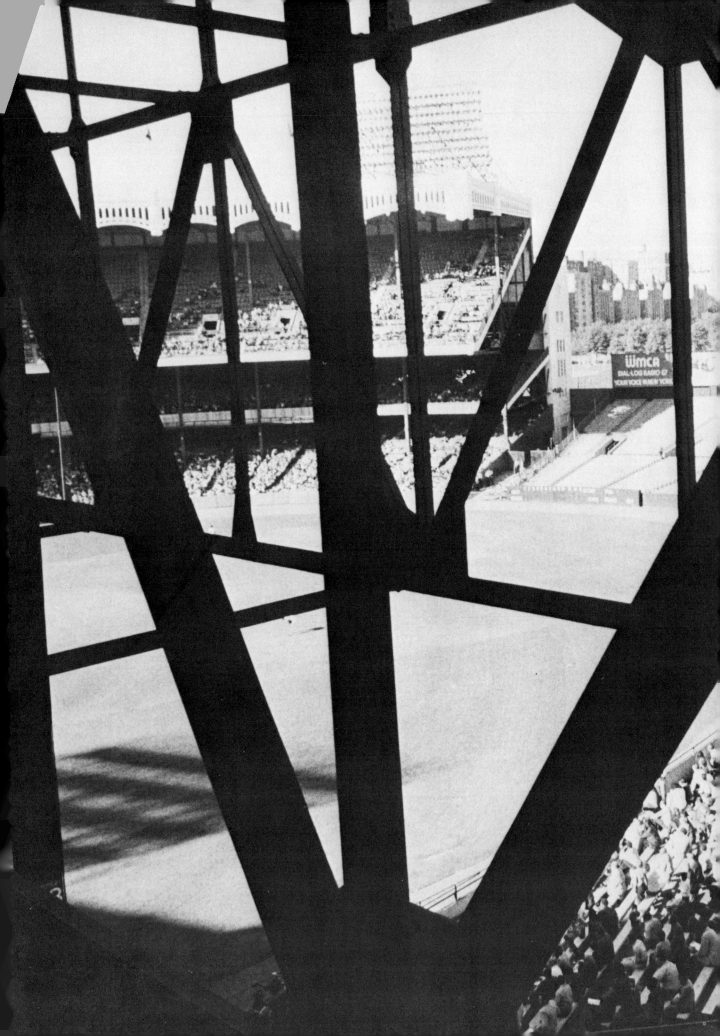

Yankee Stadium displayed a series of monuments to Yankee greats like Babe Ruth, Lou
Gehrig, manager Miller Huggins, and club president Edward Barrow. The monuments will be
returned to the outfield when the park reconstruction is completed. In the original park, they
were within the playing field but over 450 feet
from the plate and seldom reached by hits.
(*Photo above courtesy of New York Yankees;
photo right and on following page by George
Kalinsky*)

was the overall performance of consistency that earned the Yankees their reputation and gave Yankee Stadium its place in baseball history.

Historically a muted green, Yankee Stadium was perked up in its last years by a coat of white paint on its exterior and deep blue on its seats, pillars, and interior. It was in this condition that it was sold to the city of New York and closed for renovation after the 1973 season. After fifty-one years, the final AL game was played in the original Yankee Stadium on September 30, 1973, with the widows of two of the Yankees' greatest stars, Babe Ruth and Lou Gehrig, among the 32,238 in attendance.

The contemplation of past and future seems to be written on Joe DiMaggio's face. The reconstruction of Yankee Stadium forms a backdrop for the man who made an enormous contribution to the vast store of memories created in the original stadium. DiMaggio was chosen the greatest living baseball player in a 1969 poll conducted for the professional baseball centennial. (*Photo courtesy of UPI*)

Shea Stadium

Shea Stadium is the New York Mets, and the New York Mets are Shea Stadium. Although the Yankees shared the park as tenants in 1974 and 1975, the story of Shea Stadium is integrally intertwined with that of its resident darlings. From the bizarre to the brilliant and sometimes back again, the Mets have made the history of Shea Stadium a fascinating one ever since the park opened in 1964.

Robert Moses, New York's master builder, had been proposing a stadium in Flushing Meadow adjacent to the grounds of the 1939 to 1940 New York World's Fair for many years. The subject came up again when Walter O'Malley was attempting to persuade the New York administration of Mayor Robert Wagner to condemn land for him in downtown Brooklyn in the mid-1950s.

But theory didn't begin to become reality until 1961, when the NL granted an expansion franchise to New

The Shea Stadium environment created its own style of fans, youthful and exuberant, dubbed "the New Breed" by New York newspapers. Regrettably, their victory celebrations displayed malicious streaks of violence, often causing extensive damage to the ballpark. (*Photo right courtesy of UPI; photo below courtesy of New York Mets*)

York. A bond issue was floated for 24 million dollars, and Flushing Meadow was going to get its ballpark. While it was being built, the new Mets played two seasons in the Polo Grounds. By an interesting coincidence, Shea Stadium opened in the first year of another World's Fair in New York on the same site as the previous one.

At the Polo Grounds, the Mets compiled records of 40 wins and 120 losses in 1962 and 51 wins and 111 defeats in 1963. In the two seasons, they finished an aggregate of 109 games behind the pennant winners; they also drew 2,002,638.

With virtually the same type of record, the Mets at Shea Stadium suddenly became one of New York's top sports attractions. In 1964, their first season in the new park, they drew 1,732,597 fans. The Mets outdrew the pennant-winning Yankees by over 400,000. They also finished dead last in a ten-team league.

The move to Shea Stadium accomplished several things for the Mets from the attendance standpoint, some of them psychological. A large part of the old two-team base of National League attendance in New York was the enthusiastic, dedicated, and unforgiving Dodger fan of Brooklyn. For almost ten years the Giants and Dodgers constituted the backbone of the Mets' gate. But many Dodger fans were less than enthusiastic about going to the Polo Grounds, home for decades of the hated Giants. Shea Stadium was also more convenient for most people in Queens and Brooklyn who followed the Dodgers. The presence of the World's Fair pulled millions of tourists out to the railroad and subway stations that lay between the Fair Grounds and Shea Stadium. At least a few wandered in to watch the already famous Mets perform their baseball comedy act.

Just when all of the novelty might have been wearing a bit thin, the Mets suddenly turned into a winner. The "Miracle Mets" of 1969 under manager Gil Hodges, himself formerly both a Dodger hero and an original Met, shot up from ninth place (twenty-four games behind St. Louis) to first in the East Division. The Atlanta Braves were eliminated in three straight games, and there were the Mets in the World Series against the powerful Baltimore Orioles. New York went slightly bananas.

Slightly bananas turned into completely bananas as the Series itself was played out. Opening in Baltimore, the Mets were beaten by the favored Orioles, 4–1, on October 11 in game one. The next day, the Mets won

2–1 and tied the set at a game apiece. Then came a day for "travel."

On October 14 at Shea Stadium, the first NL World Series game in New York since 1956 was played. The Mets won it 5–0. They took the final two games, 2–1 and 5–3, and became world champions. Sensational outfield catches by Ron Swoboda and Tommy Agee, heavy hitting by Don Clendenon, and timely pitching made it for the Mets.

In the afterglow of their incredible victory, attendance at Shea broke the two million mark for the second straight season with a club record 2,697,479 in 1970, highest single-season total in New York baseball. Shea Stadium immediately became a place to be. Another pennant in 1973 under rookie manager Yogi Berra brought night game World Series action to Shea. Rusty Staub did some outstanding hitting against the Oakland A's, especially at Shea, but the A's outlasted the Mets in the seven-game Series.

As anyone who attended the Series games in 1973 can tell you, a night game at Shea Stadium in October can be a chilling experience. Set next to Flushing Bay, Shea is open on the water side and highly susceptible to cold winds both early and late in the season. It is also an uncovered stand, which adds to the wind's authority. The open center-field area combines with the high stands to create a funnel for the winds to swirl around in, creating sometimes tricky currents for outfielders on high fly balls.

(*Photos courtesy of UPI*)

Shea Stadium is named for William A. Shea, a New York attorney who was extremely active in the efforts to get a National League team in New York after the Giants and Dodgers moved to California in 1957. The franchise is owned by Mrs. Joan Whitney Payson, a former shareholder in the Giants when they were based in New York. She was represented on the board of directors of the Giants by M. Donald Grant, now chairman of the board of the Mets.

Yet it was the Dodgers who set the regular season attendance record at Shea with a doubleheader in 1965. The capacity of the park is 55,101 for baseball, as it has been since it opened. The dimensions have also remained the same, 341 feet down each line and 410 feet to center. The Mets have added a unique feature, however, in that they have distance measurement signs outside playing boundaries. Beyond the fences in center is a screen that runs around the edge of the parking lot. Affixed to this, the scoreboard in right center, and a utility building are distance markers.

While football is a regular attraction at Shea, the New York Jets having played there since 1964 and the Giants joining them in 1975, baseball is the dominant event in the park. When it was designed, Moses considered soccer to be a coming sport in America, and the concept of placing the lower box seats on rails for movement into sideline positions was as much for that purpose as for football.

For a ballpark of the superstadium era, Shea Stadium is somewhat on the conservative side. No flashing scoreboard, wild sound effects, or fireworks—just baseball on grass. The approach to the game here is traditional, the modern effects (escalators, etc.) being confined to the stands.

Oakland

In 1967, when Charles Finley announced that his Athletics were moving from Kansas City to Oakland, the folks in the Bay Area hardly knew what they were in for.

Since the A's arrival in Oakland, their followers have been treated to a steady succession of public spats that rival the Hollywood of the 1940s. Even more surprising has been the brand of baseball turned in by the Oakland club, which has produced three successive world championships.

Built in 1965, the Oakland Coliseum (formally known as the Oakland-Alameda County Coliseum) is a two-building complex which was used for almost everything except baseball before Finley's big switch. Adjoining the ballpark is an area of the same name which houses pro basketball, NHL hockey, ice shows, and similar events. The Oakland Raiders of the American Football Conference have made their home in the Coliseum, outdoor version, since it opened.

Of the 47,233 paying customers who showed up for the first major league baseball game in Oakland, few suspected that they would be back in less than five years for a World Series in the same ballpark. Oakland fans over the years had their share of outstanding baseball, mainly through the work of Brick Laws, guiding light behind the triple-A Oakland Oaks of the Pacific Coast League. The Oaks, who played in the 11,200-seat Oaks Park for many years, turned in some outstanding clubs including one in 1948 which was managed to the PCL pennant by one Casey Stengel. It was that job that enabled Stengel to move to the Yankees.

The Oaks ceased operating in 1958 when the Giants moved into San Francisco and claimed the territory in the Bay Area for the major leagues. San Francisco had an unchallenged hold on the entire region until the A's arrival. The drawing power of the Oakland club has since split the market and left the Giants struggling, their attendance now the lowest in the National League. The A's haven't really done that much better with their half of the market. In their first seven seasons at the Oakland Coliseum, the A's have drawn over one million only once (in 1973) and that just barely. Their total attendance averages 863,230 per season. And that was accomplished with four division champions and three World Series winners. The quality of the team would seem to deserve stronger support.

The Coliseum itself is something like a concrete pillbox. The field seems to sit down in a well below the level of the stands and gives the impression of being an extremely hot place to play. The A's generally play most of their weekday games at night, but most Saturdays and, of course, Sundays are day games. The field is surrounded in the outfield by an 8-foot high wall. The field dimensions are symmetrical, 330 down each line, 375 into both power alleys and 400 to straightaway center. However, the distances are somewhat deceiving. The air seems heavy in the Coliseum, and balls don't carry well. This makes Reggie Jackson's forty-seven-homer performance in 1969 even more remarkable. Wind is not much of a factor in the bowllike confines of the Coliseum, but the sun can be treacherous at certain

imes of the day, as the 1973 World Series indicated quite clearly.

Located south of downtown Oakland, the Coliseum is extremely convenient to southern residential suburbs such as Hayward, an area from which the A's seem to draw a lot of their fans. Public transportation to the immediate vicinity of the Coliseum is not outstanding, but travel by car over the Nimitz Freeway is rapid and usually uncongested during regular ballgame times.

Charlie Finley runs probably the tightest ship in the major leagues and the entire Coliseum operation appears to be economic, bordering on sparse. Befitting this atmosphere, the Coliseum itself is a trim building with no frills and seemingly devoid of personality.

But the A's have more than made up for any deficiency in this area. Their flamboyance in recent seasons has included long holdouts, court cases, defaulted contracts, verbal battles with the owner, physical battles with teammates, and the famous "firing" incident involving Mike Andrews in the 1973 World Series.

Yet, through it all, the A's have become the strongest team in the majors during the mid-1970s, dispatching Cincinnati, the Mets, and Los Angeles in successive World Series to become the first team since 1953 to win as many as three Series in a row. Stars of the A's since the move from Kansas City have rivaled the great clubs of Connie Mack nearly a half-century earlier during the Philadelphia incarnation of the Athletics. Outfielders Reggie Jackson, Joe Rudi, and Bill North, third baseman Sal Bando, pitchers Vida Blue, Ken Holtzman, and Catfish Hunter—now with the Yankees—were among the standouts on the championship A's clubs.

Except during the World Series, the Oakland Coliseum is seldom filled. Its capacity for baseball is 48,621, stacked basically into three decks. About one-third of that capacity is in the lower deck. Atop that are another 1,488 loge boxes and then the second tier with its 11,219 seats. The third deck has 13,537 seats in the open, unroofed top of the ballpark. The final 7,000 seats are in the outfield bleacher sections.

On October 14, 1973, one of the most bizarre games in the World Series history was played in the Coliseum. It was the second game of the Series between the Mets and the A's. It was a game that left the partisans in the crowd of 49,151 alternately screaming for glee and weeping in pain for over four hours. The twelve-inning marathon was finally decided by a four-run outburst by the Mets in the final inning. Oakland scored two runs in the first inning, led 3–1 after two, 3–2 after three, trailed 6–3 after six, cut it to 6–4, and then finally tied the game in the last of the ninth, 6–6.

The Mets had Bud Harrelson thrown out in a close play at the plate in the tenth and finally broke the deadlock when Willie Mays singled to center with two out and Harrelson at third. Two errors by Mike Andrews set up three more New York runs and rendered the A's run in the home twelfth meaningless. But the hysteria was all in a day's work for the A's, and they eventually won the Series in seven games.

Simplistic styling is the mark of the Oakland–Alameda County Coliseum. Its simple concrete construction is embellished by plain board seats and, often, by smallish crowds. (*Photo courtesy of Oakland–Alameda County Coliseum*)

Philadelphia

Philadelphia came of age as a baseball city in 1866, when the Athletics won their first national championship. It blossomed into full-blown enthusiasm for the game two years later when the A's repeated the trick.

When the National Association was formed into the first competitive league in 1871, the Athletics reigned as the league champions. They won the flag by beating Chicago on October 30 at Brooklyn's Union Grounds. The game was moved to Brooklyn because Chicago's park was destroyed by the Chicago fire. But there was no doubt among Athletics' adherents that they would have won the pennant no matter where the decisive game was played.

Much to the surprise of Philadelphia's baseball cranks, Boston won the next four successive pennants. But by this time G. W. Thompson's club was no longer alone in the city. A second team, known as Philadelphia, joined the NA in 1873 and finished second while the embarrassed A's fell to fourth. By 1875 a third club, the Centennials, were in the NA as Philadelphia representatives. But when the National League was formed in 1876, Thomas J. Smith, then the club president, moved them into the new circuit as the sole Philadelphia entrant.

The first NL game ever played took place at the A's grounds at 29th Street and Jefferson Avenue on April 22, 1876, other games scheduled for that day being rained out. Boston again took the measure of the Athletics, winning 6–5. But further trouble came at the end of the season when the A's followed the lead of William Cammeyer's New York Mutuals and refused to make their final journeys to the west.

When William Hulbert assumed the presidency of the NL at the end of that year, Philadelphia found itself expelled from the circuit along with New York. But unlike the Mutuals, who eventually disbanded, the Athletics continued to play. When the American Association was organized as a rival to the NL in 1882, they were among the charter clubs. After a third-place finish in the first year of the AA, the Athletics returned to their championship form and won the flag in 1883. That same year, they got competition for the affection of the Philadelphia fans. A former local star player and sporting goods dealer, Alfred J. Reach, purchased the moribund Worcester, Massachusetts, club in the NL and had no trouble getting permission to move it to Philadelphia.

Reach set up his club at Recreation Park on Ridge Avenue between 24th and 25th streets and played his first home game there on May 1, 1883. Like most other NL teams that year, the new Phillies ran into Charlie Radbourn and lost their home opener to Providence 4–3.

During the next half dozen years, the two local clubs became friendly rivals and played each other on off days and before and after the regular season. Neither won a championship during those years. In 1890, the Players League war hit Philadelphia. But both local clubs survived well. After the war was over, the backers of the PL team, George and J. Earle Wagner, brought the Athletics and moved them to their grounds at 35th and Dauphin.

Al Reach had already solved his ballpark problem by building Baker Bowl at Broad and Huntingdon in 1887. The original grandstand from the right-field corner to the left-field corner in this park was the first cantilevered stand in baseball. It had a wooden bleacher in the outfield from the left-field line to center field where it angled toward right center and joined a wall about thirty feet high which for many years was dominated by a huge sign advertising A. J. Reach Sporting Goods.

Baker Bowl, as it came to be called much later, opened on April 30, 1887, with a game against the Giants who were, by a quirk of the schedule, to close it fifty-one years later. The inaugural was attended by a capacity crowd of 18,000 who saw the Phils slam the Giants 15–9 after scoring nine runs in the first inning off Giant ace Tim Keefe. The game was called after seven innings due to darkness, wiping out four more Phillie runs in the top of the eighth.

Reach's ballpark was the pride of Philadelphia when it was built, though a half century later it may have been the most outmoded park in baseball. When it opened, Baker Bowl was 335 feet to left, 408 to center, and 272 to right. Sam Thompson attacked the 272-foot right-field fence for the then impressive figure of twenty homers in 1889, the third full season in the park.

In 1894 a plumber's stove started a fire in the park while the team was practicing on August 6. The main stands were completely destroyed at a loss of $80,000 to the club. A hasty rebuilding job led to an eventual renovation in 1896 which cost $40,000 and left the capacity at 16,000 plus another 4,000 standing room. A disaster of even more serious consequences struck the park seven years later.

During a game in August 1903 fans became interested in a fight on Fifteenth Street outside Baker Bowl. Many of them crowded against the railing at the top of the stands. Suddenly, the stands collapsed, throwing dozens of fans onto the street, killing twelve and injuring another hundred. Heavy litigation followed this tragedy, and the park was closed while repairs were made.

Since 1901, when the American League extended itself to the east, the Phillies had a local rival once more —Connie Mack and his Athletics. The new A's were housed in Columbia Park at 29th Street and Columbia Avenue. After the Baker Bowl disaster, the Phils were accorded the use of the grounds for their games while the repairs were made at Broad and Huntingdon, courtesy of Ben Shibe and Mack, co-owner of the AL club.

Columbia Park was a single-deck wooden affair with a covered stand extending behind the plate from first base to third and open bleachers going down the foul lines. A small press box was perched atop the roof behind the plate. The A's, however, were quite pleased when they drew 206,329 into it in 1901, only about 30,000 less than the established Phillies did in the same season. The A's gate doubled in 1902 when they won their first pennant and climbed even higher in 1905 when they finished first again. Shibe and Mack began planning to build a new home for their team.

The Phillies, meanwhile, returned to Baker Bowl and, in 1915, rode the strong arm of Grover Cleveland Alexander to their first modern pennant. Although the Phils lost the Series to Boston in five games, they achieved a distinction when the second game at Baker Bowl attracted President Wilson and Mrs. Edith Bolling Galt, later Mrs. Wilson.

Alexander performed one of the miraculous feats in baseball history during his seven-year career with the Phils. Pitching in the tight confines of Baker Bowl, he posted records of 28–13, 19–17, 22–8, 27–15, 31–10, 33–12, and 30–13 between 1911 and 1917, leading the league in strikeouts four straight years, in lowest earned run average three times, and winning percentage once in the process. In 1918 he was traded to the Cubs. In later years, the brilliant Alexander gained a reputation for drinking a bit. Pitching in a park with a 272-foot fence, it's no wonder.

In an era when concrete and steel ballparks were springing up left and right, the Phils and their owner, Gerry Nugent, doggedly stayed with their decaying Baker Bowl. Its capacity of 18,800 included some 2,000 box seats, 2,500 field stand reserved seats, 12,300 grandstand seats, and 2,000 bleachers. Considering the quality of most Phillie clubs during the 1920s and 1930s, there were plenty of seats. The plate was moved slightly, amending the distances to 280 to right and 341 to left.

Finally, in 1938, Nugent reached an agreement with Mack to move into Shibe Park. The final series in Baker Bowl included a doubleheader on June 29, which the Giants swept, 9–1 and 6–2, and the last game on June 30 in which New York avenged its humiliation of a half-century earlier, 14–1. Baker Bowl, a signal piece of

Baker Bowl, as it became popularly known, was the forerunner of the modern ballparks when opened in 1887, and crowds of 15,000, huge for the time, were not uncommon. After it was abandoned, plans were discussed to build an indoor sports arena on the site but the arena never materialized. Above is the handy right-field wall seen from Broad Street. (*Photo courtesy of Wide World*)

architecture when it opened, was abandoned as a ancient relic. During its final years only the batting prowess of Chuck Klein excited interest among Phillie fans.

Connie Mack Stadium (Shibe Park)

When the final series between the A's and the Red Sox wrapped up the 1908 home season in Philadelphia at Columbia Park, the Athletics' fans were already buzzing about the prospect of the new Shibe Park set to open the following spring. Baseball was to get its first concrete and steel ballpark, and the A's were going to have it.

The gala day arrived on April 12, 1909. The first ticket purchaser, George McFadden, arrived at 7:00 A.M. and stood in front of the grandstand gate until it opened at 12:15. Before the game began at shortly after 3:00 P.M., AL president Ban Johnson assisted A's president Shibe in the flag raising, and Mayor John E. Rey-

burn threw out the first ball. Among those in the audience was George Wright, great shortstop of two national championship teams in the 1860s. Wright said of the occasion, "It is the most remarkable sight I have ever witnessed." The paid attendance was 30,162, but an estimated 5,000 more were invited guests or gatecrashers. Additional thousands bought space on rooftops around the park for up to three dollars a head. Fortunately, given the excited state of this huge turnout, the A's beat the Red Sox handily 8–1 behind Eddie Plank.

The attendance for the first season at Shibe Park was 674,915, a total not exceeded by the A's until 1925. Construction had begun with a groundbreaking one day less than a year before. The end product was a stand in two decks that held 7,000, a bleacher down the line in left with a capacity for another 7,000, and one down the right field for an additional 6,000.

The additional crowd, some 10,000 on opening day, was accommodated in the outfield, standing on graded slopes in front of the walls. The original dimensions of 360 feet down the lines, 395 feet into the power alleys, and 420 to center field allowed for this practice in the dead ball days.

A unique innovation at Shibe Park was the installation of garages under the bleachers in left and right, each garage holding 200 1909-style cars. The entire park was surrounded by a wall eight feet high.

OUR REDS DO IT THE HARD WAY LOVE MARGE

New ballparks are often sites for unique but less-than-new
expressions of human activity. A Cincinnati fan provides
Riverfront Stadium with an airborne message, while
Philadelphia's Veterans Stadium launches its own airborne
communications. The scoreboard is quietly telling its story in
Cincinnati. (*Photo above and photo below left by George
Kalinsky; photo below right courtesy of Philadelphia Phillies*)

Although often similar in concept, the new ballparks
do have some individual style of their own and,
as in these shots from Riverfront Stadium, they
sometimes even give you something to reflect about.
(*Photos by George Kalinsky*)

Veterans Stadium, Philadelphia, a triumvirate with its neighbors the Spectrum and Kennedy Stadium (not shown), provides the backdrop for the promotion-conscious Phillies with their Hot Pants Patrol and club record attendance in 1974. (*Photo courtesy of Philadelphia Phillies*)

Separated by an entire continent, San Diego Stadium and New York's Shea Stadium are united by the greatness of Willie Mays. In the shot below Mays is batting for the Mets during his farewell year. Both as a Giant and Met, Mays was a frequent visitor in San Diego. (*Photos left courtesy of San Diego Padres; photo below by George Kalinsky*)

Metropolitan Stadium in Bloomington, Minnesota, is situated
between the twin cities, Minneapolis and St. Paul and gives the
baseball Twins a draw from both areas, hopefully thereby
avoiding bruised civic pride in either city. (*Photo courtesy*

Included in the epidemic of new ballparks constructed since 1965 are
(*above*) Houston's Astrodome and (*below*) Pittsburgh's Three Rivers Stadium.
Also, Anaheim Stadium (*facing page, upper left*); Atlanta Stadium (*upper
right*); and the older, privately owned Dodger Stadium in Los Angeles (*bottom*).
(*Photos courtesy of Houston Astros, Pittsburgh Pirates, California Angels,
Atlanta Braves, and Los Angeles Dodgers*)

Behind home plate in Candlestick Park is Giants
Way, a street named for the team during happier
days for both the club and the city. Meanwhile,
at Shea Stadium, the crowd heads out after a game
in the city the Giants left behind. (*Photos by
George Kalinsky*)

Columbia Park was built by Ben Shibe and Connie Mack for the AL Athletics in 1901. However, Shibe and Mack soon began laying plans for a concrete park and broke ground for what became Shibe Park on April 13, 1908. The plan was to overshadow Baker Bowl and it succeeded so well that the NL club eventually moved in as tenant. (*Photo courtesy of Baseball Hall of Fame; Baker Bowl photos left and next page courtesy of UPI*)

The A's finished second in 1909 but won four pennants in the next five seasons, 1910, 1911, 1913, and 1914, with an outstanding club which included Plank, Eddie Collins, Frank (Homerun) Baker, and Chief Bender. Jack Barry at short and Stuffy McInnis, along with Collins at second and Baker at third, comprised the "$100,000 infield" of Mack's champions.

In 1913 the first major changes were made in Shibe Park, the uncovered stands being roofed over and a bleacher being added across left field right to the flagpole in center. In 1925 a second deck was added from behind first base to the right-field corner and from just past third all the way around to left and across to center, enclosing three-quarters of the park.

In 1929 Mack started another string of winning teams. The A's won pennants in 1929, 1930, and 1931. A mezzanine section of 2,500 seats was added to the park in 1929 and the next year the roof of the original main stand was raised to add another 3,000 seats.

During this era the great A's included the "$1,000,-000 Infield" of Jimmy Foxx, Max Bishop, John Boley, and Jimmy Dykes, from first to third. In the outfield the A's had Mule Haas, Al Simmons, and Bing Miller. The catcher was Mickey Cochran and the pitching stars were Bob (Lefty) Grove and George Earnshaw. Some observers are of the opinion that the 1931 edition may have been the greatest team of all time—the 1927 Yankees notwithstanding—despite their loss to St. Louis in the World Series.

The 1929 Series produced one of the highlights of post-season history. The A's won the first two games in Chicago, but the Cubs took game three at Shibe Park. In the fourth game, October 12, 1929, the Cubs were on their way to equalizing the Series. Chicago scored two runs in the fourth and five more in the sixth. They added another in the top of the seventh and led 8–0 when the A's came to bat. Simmons opened the inning with a homer. Before Chicago could get three outs, Haas got credit for a three-run inside-the-park homer when Hack Wilson misjudged his fly; the A's got ten hits, a walk, and a hit batsman; sent fifteen men to the plate; and scored ten runs—the largest inning in World Series history. The A's won the game 10–8. The exhausted Cubs were as good as dead and the A's closed out the Series the next afternoon.

In 1934 the right-field wall was raised from twelve

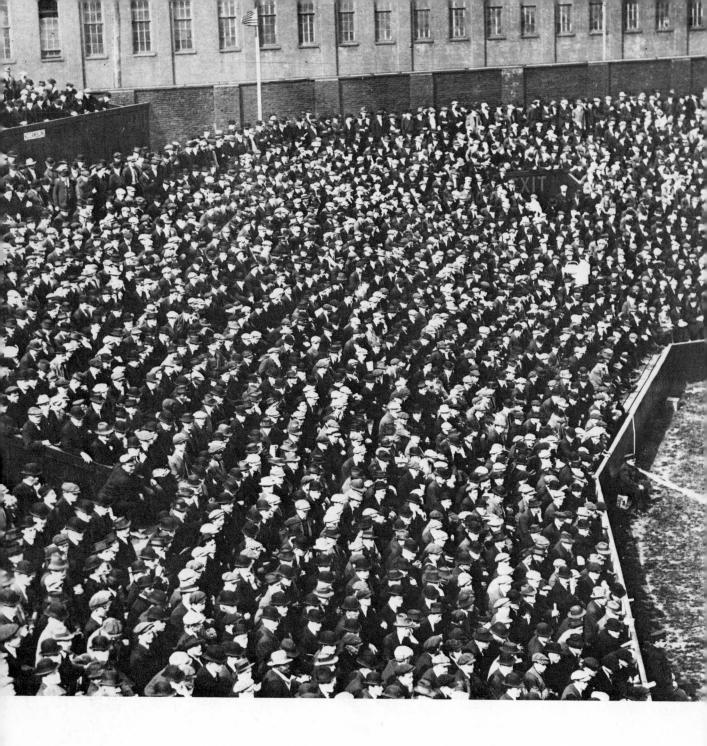

Shibe Park, renamed Connie Mack Stadium in 1953, was a palace of baseball in its time. During their years there, the Phillies outlasted the A's and replaced them as the park's owners. The final game turned into near-riot and over two dozen fans were injured, another suffering a stroke on the left-field grass. A fire burned part of the park in August 1971. *(Photos on pages 183, 184, and 186 courtesy of UPI)*

feet to fifty feet and the number of homers in Shibe Park dropped sharply. Mack made the move primarily because he was in the process of selling off his stars for cash and didn't want visiting teams to clobber his club.

Economics also played its part in the next major alterations in the Shibe Park scene. On July 4, 1938, the Phillies moved from their Baker Bowl home a few blocks down Lehigh Street into Shibe Park and split a doubleheader with the Boston Braves. They were to remain thirty-two years.

In 1939 light towers went up on Shibe Park's roof. At the time only two parks in the majors (Cincinnati and Brooklyn) had lights, both having them installed by Larry MacPhail. Smug AL owners had stayed aloof from the after dark ballgame idea. But Mack gave it a try, and on May 16 the A's played the first night game in AL history against Cleveland, losing 8–3 in ten innings.

In 1941 a new scoreboard was installed in right field and the field dimensions stood at 334 to left, 468 to center, and 331 to right. The capacity remained at 33,000. After the war, a complete face-lifting was given to the park, the original flagstone being replaced by granite, the entire park being repaired, the brick painted and the pillars cleaned. In 1948 the lower stands were turned toward the plate and box seats were extended down toward the foul poles. In 1949 the pitching of

Robin Roberts and Curt Simmons started to make the Phillies a contender for the first time in decades. During their final full season at Baker Bowl, the Phils drew a meager 212,790. Splitting the 1938 season between Baker Bowl and Shibe Park, the total had actually dropped; it hit 166,111. But it began slowly to creep upward as the team improved and in 1946, the Phils hit the million-mark for the first time.

In 1950 the famed "Whiz Kids" won a pennant and 2,026,840 fans spun through the Shibe Park turnstiles, 1,217,035 to Phils games and 809,805 to A's. On the final day of the season at Brooklyn, Dick Sisler lofted an opposite-field three-run homer in the tenth inning to give the Phillies a victory and a pennant for the first time since 1915. Roberts, Simmons, relief artist Jim Konstanty, Willie (Puddin' Head) Jones, Richie Ashburn, Sisler, Eddie Waitkus, and Granny Hammer became heroes overnight. The fact that they got swept in four games by the Yankees in the series was almost insignificant to their excited fans.

But the Phils gradually faded and so did the A's, even more so after Connie Mack ended fifty years as the team's manager following the 1950 season. The name of the park was changed to Connie Mack Stadium to honor the still living Mack in 1953.

But the A's were gone from Connie Mack Stadium after the 1954 season, moved off to Kansas City and,

eventually, to Oakland. The Phils bought the old park and shortened the center field to 447 feet. In 1956 they bought the electric scoreboard from Yankee Stadium and installed it in right field, reducing the wall to thirty-two feet in height at the same time.

During its final fifteen seasons, Connie Mack Stadium had a heavy red hue with its box seats and railings all painted bright red which contrasted sharply with the green of the grass. Virtually all of the Phillies' games were played at night, except Sundays, giving the park an identity virtually divorced from its dingy surroundings in North Philadelphia. The exterior architecture of the main entranceway was French Renaissance garnished by layers of paint, like a vain woman hiding her years with only minimal success.

But with all of the signs of age, Connie Mack Stadium—like all of the older parks—gave a feeling of intimacy even from the upper deck seats, and it was a cozy place to watch a ballgame.

In 1964, when the Phillies were hurtling toward a pennant only to be derailed in September, 1,425,891 fans poured into the park, a club record. It went slowly down to 708,247 by 1970 when the park closed after sixty-two years on October 1. It was a wild night in which 31,822 fans paid their last respects, and many began the demolition job early. Some also decided to bid the players farewell before the game ended, nearly bringing on a forfeit. A single by Oscar Gamble sent home Tim McCarver with a tenth-inning run which gave the Phillies a 2–1 victory.

Some 47 million fans watched baseball at Shibe Park during the forty-six years the AL played there and the thirty-two years it was used by the NL. The two leagues shared the park for sixteen seasons (1938 to 1954), and the night it closed Shibe Park was the oldest ballpark in the majors in continuous use.

Veterans Stadium

A new era came to Philadelphia baseball on April 10, 1971, when the city of Shibe Park, Connie Mack, Robin Roberts, Baker Bowl, and Brotherly Love opened its Veterans Stadium for the first time.

Though much like many of its contemporaries in overall concept and design, the Phillies worked hard to make Veterans Stadium something different among ballparks. Disregarding the unfortunate AstroTurf and the cut-out style infield with no base paths, Veterans Stadium can be a worthwhile park to visit.

The calendar of special activities is, if anything, overloaded at the Vet. Wirewalkers and helicopter drops are on the program right along with baseball. Also available are a wide variety of heavily promoted package plans that utilize the Vet facilities. Among the choices are "Base Hit" (group ticket plan), "Double Play" (a box seat plus a box lunch), "Pinch Hitter" (box seat and bring your own lunch), "The Round Tripper," and an evening at the "Grand Slam Room."

The Phillies have picnic areas in either corner which are utilized for many of these special packages. The club also operates railroad excursions from as far away as Harrisburg and Lancaster in conjunction with big promotions (like Team Shirt Day, Cap Day, Wrist Band Day, Bat Day, T-Shirt Day, Ball Day).

With an improvement in the club helping out, Phillie attendance at the Vet has been impressive in the first four seasons. In 1974 it hit a club record of 1,808,693.

Structurally, the Vet is shaped like a square with its corners rounded off. Its exterior is dominated by vertical columns from ground level to the roof. Inside, the scoreboards are quite likely to catch your attention. There are two of them, each 100 feet by 25 feet, in the outfield plus two auxiliary boards, 90 feet by 13 feet. Three of the four are animated and flash cartoons and messages in color throughout the game. Sometimes, just a little too often.

Rather surprisingly, Veterans Stadium has the second largest ballpark capacity in the National League with 56,581 seats. This capacity includes 254 super boxes and 1,004 deluxe boxes sold on a season basis. It also includes 8,957 field boxes, 8,800 terrace boxes, 5,711 loge boxes, 17,979 upper level reserved seats, and 13,876 general admission. The seats are numbered by level from the deluxe boxes (100 series) up to the upper general admission (700 series). About 70 percent of the seats are in foul territory, the balance in the outfield upper stands.

The Vet is situated in a complex of Philadelphia facilities which include the John F. Kennedy Stadium, site of the annual Army-Navy football game, and the Spectrum, the city's principal indoor arena. All three share parking and other support services and transit connec-

Veterans Stadium in south Philadelphia is located in a three-building complex that includes John F. Kennedy Stadium and the Spectrum. Home plate in the new ballpark was transplanted from Shibe Park after the old park closed in 1970. (*Photos right, page 185, and pages 190–191 courtesy of Philadelphia Phillies*)

tions via Pattison Avenue on the Broad Street subway.

The playing dimensions of the Vet are 330 feet down each line, 371 into the power alleys in left- and right-center, and 408 to dead center field. The outfield fences are now 12 feet high all the way around. The fences had to be raised during the first season (1971) because so many balls bounced off the hard AstroTurf and bounded over the fences.

Pittsburgh

After the Players League war ended in 1890, all players were expected to return to the clubs for which they had played in 1889. Louis Bierbauer, a second baseman with Brooklyn in the PL, went to Pittsburgh of the NL for the 1891 season. Since he had spent the previous four seasons with the Philadelphia Athletics in the American Association, the A's and their AA brethren immediately began screaming "pirates" at the Pittsburgh club.

Since Pittsburgh had jumped the AA into the NL in 1887, there was already bad blood between the club and the remaining Association members, so Pittsburgh kept Bierbauer. As a result, they also kept the tag "Pirates," and became known as the Pittsburgh Pirates for ever after.

The previous history of Pittsburgh baseball had revolved primarily around the Allegheny club which was to become the Pirates. The Allegheny Club utilized Pittsburgh's first enclosed ballpark, Union Park, on April 15, 1876, when it played the opening game in the short-lived International Association. Having not been a member of the National Association, Pittsburgh wasn't invited to join the new NL that season and had to wait until 1882, when the AA began, to enter a stable organization.

Pittsburgh serves as an excellent example of the flexibility of ballpark usage during the wooden park epoch. Upon joining the AA, the Allegheny built Exposition Park at the confluence of the Allegheny and Monongahela rivers, virtually on the site of today's Three Rivers Stadium. When the franchise jumped into the National League, the club moved to the more modern Recreation Park.

This park, located in a plot bounded by Grant, Allegheny, and Pennsylvania avenues and the Ft. Wayne Railroad yards, was originally constructed for the Union Association team which had invaded the Pittsburgh territory in 1884.

In 1890 the PL club did some renovation on Exposition Park, a somewhat larger stand than Recreation Park. After the war ended in 1891, the Pirates moved back to their former home at Exposition Park. They remained their until mid-1909, when the shift to Forbes Field was made.

Competitively, the Allegheny club was hardly the scourge of the AA. In the charter season of 1882, Pittsburgh finished fourth. But the league had only six clubs at that point, and Pittsburgh had to struggle to split even at thirty-nine wins and thirty-nine losses for the year. In 1883, they sank to seventh among eight and then to eleventh among twelve finishers in 1884. Then things began to improve—up to third in 1885 and second behind St. Louis the following year. Then it was that club president William A. Nimick determined to break from the AA and move into the NL. Pittsburgh became the first AA club to jump to the National League, though several others (including Brooklyn and Cincinnati) were to follow suit in subsequent seasons.

In the NL Pittsburgh was a perennial also-ran, finishing eighth four times, seventh three times, sixth four times, fifth once, and second once (1893) in the thirteen seasons from its entry into the NL and 1900. Then

Exposition Park, located near the site of Three Rivers Stadium, and shown here just before the turn of the century, twice served as the home of early Pirate clubs. On the final day, a bugler played taps and the crowd of nearly 6,000 fans stood bareheaded in respect as the flag was lowered for the final time here in 1909. (*Photos above and following page courtesy of Pittsburgh Pirates*)

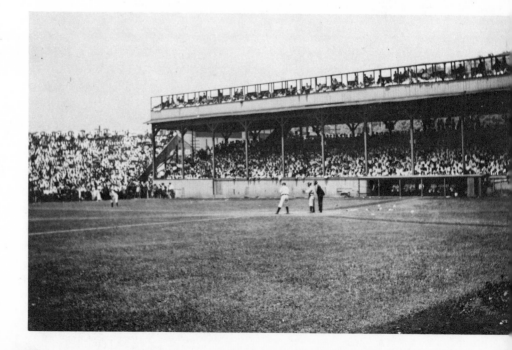

came the contraction of the circuit from twelve clubs to eight, the replacement of W. W. Kerr by Barney Dreyfuss as Pirate president, and the merging of the Louisville players into the Pirate roster. Suddenly, Pittsburgh was a contender.

In 1890 the Pirates had been demolished by the Players League and staggered through a 23–113 season. Now the tables were turned and Pittsburgh was to be bolstered by outstanding talent from an outside source. In 1900, with former Louisville manager Fred Clarke at the helm, Pittsburgh spurted from seventh the previous season to second. In 1901 the Pirates won their first pennant. The next season Pittsburgh took its second straight pennant, finishing a whooping twenty-seven and a half games in front of runnerup Brooklyn, the largest margin in NL history.

A third straight pennant followed in 1903 plus the right to represent the senior circuit in the first World Series against the new American League and its Boston Red Sox. Dreyfuss was an anxious for the Series and, in fact, arranged it with Boston's president Henry J. Killilea without the involvement of the respective league heads.

Pittsburgh, built around Honus Wagner (one of the former Louisville stars), remained a contender for the next few years, but never won another pennant in Exposition Park. Meanwhile, Dreyfuss, in the vanguard of the concrete and steel thinkers, began planning for a new park. He negotiated for the use of a piece of land adjoining Schenley Park from steel capitalist Andrew Carnegie, signed a contract with the Nicola Building Company of Pittsburgh, and, on March 1, 1909, saw ground broken for the new home of the Pirates. Among his other motivations, Dreyfuss was anxious to get out of the wooden box at Exposition Park that had been struck by flood and winds which ripped off its roof in 1900 and 1901. The twin-spired wooden park had almost told its tale.

Forbes Field

Forbes Field was the first park in the National League expressly built from scratch for baseball out of concrete and steel. Its opening on June 30, 1909, was a major civic event in Pittsburgh, and attracted the largest crowd ever to see a baseball game in the city up to that time, 30,338.

The majority of the crowd went home disappointed at the outcome of the game, won by the Chicago Cubs 3–2, but thrilled at the new addition to the city's pride. Johnny Evers of the Cubs' famed double play combination started the game with a single, and the message was significant. In the over 4,700 games played at Forbes Field during its sixty-two-season career, no pitcher ever threw a no-hitter from its mound.

Celebrated from the outset for its architectural beauty and imposing size, Forbes Field was massive by the then prevailing standards of ballparks and in some respects it was even more impressive than Philadelphia's Shibe Park which had opened at the start of the same season.

Baseball history of all kinds was to be made at Forbes Field, and it started early. The Pirates won the last of their four pennants under Fred Clarke that season and met Detroit and Ty Cobb in the World Series. Babe Adams, an almost unknown rookie, hurled three victories against the Tigers, and Pittsburgh took the Series in seven games.

Games of extreme length were to be played there, starting with the twenty-one-inning affair on July 17, 1914, when the Giants outlasted the Pirates 3–1.

When originally opened, Forbes Field measured 376 feet 6 inches down the right-field line. That was to change radically in 1925 when the big double-decked stand which was to become something of a Pittsburgh hallmark was constructed, cutting the mileage down to an even 300 feet. The rest of the ballpark remained spacious. It was 462 feet to center in those days and 360 down the line in left. Over the years, movement of the plate and the addition of some seats in the main grandstand were to alter the center and left figures slightly, but they always remained healthy even during the period of the so-called Greenberg Gardens or Kiner's Korner following the second World War.

In 1932 Dreyfuss died and his son-in-law Bill Benswanger became the president of the Pirates, with George Gibson as the field manager. On May 25, 1935, a landmark day in baseball history, George Herman (Babe) Ruth hit the last three homeruns of his career. While playing for the Boston Braves, Ruth collected three long homers against the Pirates, and the third one soared over the roof of the huge right-field stand, the first ball ever to clear it completely.

In 1938 a third level of seats was added on top of the main stands, tagged "the crow's nest" by local writers. The new seats were added in anticipation of a World Series, but the Cubs snatched the pennant from the Pirates in the waning days of the season. Pittsburgh had won flags in 1925 and 1927 with teams starring the Waner brothers, Lloyd and Paul, who were nicknamed "Big and Little Poison." But the city was to be denied in 1938 and not have another shot in the post-season classic until 1960, a lapse of thirty-three years.

In 1940 lights were added to Forbes Field, making Pittsburgh the eighth park in the majors to join the night baseball movement. The first arc-light game ever at Forbes Field came on June 4, when the Pirates blasted the Boston Braves 14–2.

After the end of World War II, a young outfielder named Ralph Kiner joined the Pirates and teamed with former Detroit slugger Hank Greenberg. Greenberg was expected to add punch to the sluggish Pittsburgh attack. Kiner not only out-homered Greenberg, but led the NL

Forbes Field was the first NL concrete grandstand and hosted the World Series in its first season, 1909. On October 2, 1920, the last tripleheader in the majors was played here, matching the Pirates against Cincinnati. Pie Traynor, Honus Wagner, Gus Suhr, Ralph Kiner, Roberto Clemente, and the Waner brothers were among the great Pirates who played their careers here. *(Photo here and photos on pages 198–199 courtesy of UPI; aerial view preceding page courtesy of Pittsburgh Pirates)*

in four-baggers with twenty-three in 1946. At this point, the management saw a good thing and decided to shorten the dimensions a bit in left field by moving the bullpens from foul territory in the corners into the outfield. They surrounded the bullpen with a 14-foot high screen which chopped the playing field down to 335 feet down the line in left, 355 in the power alley, and 435 in center.

In 1947 Kiner smacked fifty-one homers and tied with the Giants' Johnny Mize for the NL lead. The following year he did even better, clubbing fifty-four homers, second highest total in the NL's history. Pittsburgh fans responded to his heroics by pouring through the Forbes Field turnstiles in record numbers. Despite a fourth-place finish, the Pirates drew 1,517,021 in 1948. At this point Kiner was proving the adage, "Homerun hitters drive Cadillacs" and the reason was obvious. The Pirates by this time were under new ownership. Dreyfuss's widow had sold the club in 1946 to a syndicate that included Frank McKinney, John Galbreath, Tom Johnson, and famed singer Bing Crosby. In 1950 Galbreath became the club's president when McKinney sold his 40 percent interest to the other major stockholders.

In 1953 Kiner was traded to the Chicago Cubs, and the bullpens were deemed to be more properly located in foul ground in the right- and left-field corners. This resulted in the distance down the left line growing to 365 feet again. In 1959 three rows of field and dugout-level boxes were added to the park, raising the capacity to 35,000. Those seats were shortly to be stuffed full as the new Pirates, including Bill Mazeroski, Dick Groat, Roberto Clemente, and pitchers Vernon Law and Bob Friend were to break the pennant jinx. Mazeroski's dramatic ninth-inning homer in the seventh game gave the Pirates a World Championship as well, with a hysterical 10–9 victory over the Yankees.

During the next decade Forbes Field saw the Pirates undergo another transformation with only Mazeroski and the brilliant Clemente remaining on a rebuilt team. The finale for the park was a doubleheader sweep of the Cubs on June 28, 1970, witnessed by 40,918, largest house at Forbes Field since 1956. At its end the park was still 300 feet to right, 365 to left, and 457 to the deepest part of center. It was 27 feet 8 inches to the top of the screen that protected the front of the right-field stands, 12 feet to the top of the wall the rest of the way around the outfield, and 25 feet 6 inches to clear the scoreboard in left plus another 14 feet if you happened

to hit one toward the Longine clock atop the scoreboard. The park's original little scoreboard against the center-field wall was gone, replaced by a plaque to Dreyfuss amid the ivy clinging to the old bricks.

Three Rivers Stadium

In 1970 the Pirates played their first forty home dates at Forbes Field and drew 386,907. But for the season, they managed to hit nearly 1,400,000 because the last thirty-six dates at the new Three Rivers Stadium attracted 955,040.

Mayor Joseph M. Barr made some remarks and was joined by a number of Pittsburgh celebrities and sports heroes at 11:00 A.M. on Thursday, April 25, 1968. The occasion was the ground breaking for Three Rivers Stadium. It was being constructed to replace the now ancient Forbes Field. The monument it was supplanting was built in 1909 in four months. The new park was to be over two years in the making.

It finally opened on July 16, 1970. The Pirates had lost their first game at Forbes Field sixty-one years earlier to the Cubs by a 3–2 score. They did exactly the same thing at Three Rivers, losing to the Reds 3–2.

But that was the end of any similarity between the two parks. The circular Three Rivers Stadium held 50,235 fans for baseball and was symmetrical in its configuration. It also had a synthetic surface undreamed of when Barney Dreyfuss built Forbes Field, Tartan Turf. Gone, too, were the base paths, leaving in their wake the small cut-outs or sliding pits around each of the bases. The first full season in the new stadium produced not only a pennant but a world championship.

For the All-Star Game in 1974, the ten-foot outfield wall was decorated with the emblems of all twenty-four major league clubs. They added a splash of color to an already colorful scene. In keeping with the general trend, a huge scoreboard, sandwiched in between the general admission sections, dominated the center-field segment of the park.

One aspect of Forbes Field remains in Three Rivers Stadium. The bullpens are tucked into the foul territory

United States Steel played a peculiar role in Pittsburgh ballparks. It provided steel for Forbes Field in 1909 and built Three Rivers Stadium, which replaced Forbes, in 1970. The new stadium is at the confluence of the Ohio, Allegheny, and Monongahela rivers. (*Photos here and pages 202 and 203 courtesy of Pittsburgh Pirates*)

portion of the respective corners of the playing field, behind low wooden fences.

The big open-air box sections are divided into two tiers, 8,058 in the field box area and 7,288 in the loge boxes immediately behind. On the next level, another 2,848 box seats are added plus 13,800 reserved seats and, above that level, another 17,287 general admission pews. In addition to the boxes already accounted for, there are 954 special boxes available on a season basis.

Interestingly, when the All-Star Game returned to Pittsburgh for its night presentation in 1974, it was coming back to the scene (if not the site) of the first night All-Star Game ever. That was at Forbes Field on July 11, 1944, when the Nationals beat the Americans 7–1 with Rip Sewell pitching three hitless innings for the winners.

Willie Stargell hit seven of the seventeen homers ever to clear the right-field roof at Forbes, but if he is able to loft one out of Three Rivers Stadium it will be an even bigger story. The dimensions are comfortable enough, 340 to the corners, 385 in the power alleys, and 410 to center. But the height of the building seems to make such a feat a physical impossibility. But, then, that's what they thought when Forbes Field had its right-field stands added. It took a decade, but once one man hit a ball over the roof everybody got into the action, even Ted Beard.

St. Louis

Organized baseball came to St. Louis after the Civil War and has been a mainstay of the city's social life ever since. Early games were played at Veto Park, near the current Fairgrounds Park, and at what was then known as the Grand Avenue Grounds.

In 1875 two St. Louis clubs joined the National Association, one playing at the Grand Avenue Grounds and the other at Red Stocking Park. When first used in the 1860s, the Grand Avenue site was an open lot; but it was fenced in and the first wooden stands were erected in 1871.

The first shutout in professional baseball history was pitched at Red Stocking Park on May 11, 1875, when Chicago's George Zettlein threw a three-hitter and outpitched Joseph Myles Blong of the Red Stockings, 1–0, despite a six-hit job by Blong that was considered outstanding in the days of underhand pitching. The game consumed one hour thirty-five minutes. But the Red Stockings didn't finish the season.

The Grand Avenue Grounds was left as the organized baseball center of St. Louis. When the National League was organized in 1876, St. Louis moved in as one of the original members and the first NL game in St. Louis was played on Grand Avenue on May 5, St. Louis getting a 1–0 win this time, beating Chicago.

But after the 1877 season, St. Louis dropped out of the NL, leaving the city without a major organized ball club. Al Spink, later founder of *The Sporting News*, was among those who decided to try to do something about this problem. He formed the Sportsman's Park

and Club Association. Their first task was to put the Grand Avenue park into shape.

Once the ballpark was in order, Spink and his fellows assembled a team and began to book exhibition games against the best opposition available. But baseball enthusiasm in St. Louis was too high for a diet of exhibitions. When the American Association was formed in 1882 to rival the NL, St. Louis snatched off one of the six original franchises. Under the ownership of the principal financial backer of the Park and Club Association, tavern owner Chris Van der Ahe, the St. Louis Browns were born.

They finished fifth in 1882 but moved up to second in 1883. In 1884 they encountered opposition for the affection of St. Louis baseball cranks. Henry V. Lucas was the founder of a new league, the Union Association, which was based in St. Louis, and his Maroons were the circuit's strongest club by far. They opened the season with twenty straight victories, sixteen of them in their new home at Cass Avenue and West 25th Street, and shortly made a shambles of the UA race.

The Union Association expired at the end of the first season, but the NL owners, seeing a way to strike at the growing strength of the AA, gave Lucas a St. Louis franchise in their league. For the first time, St. Louis became a two-team city in two reasonably stable leagues. Although he had called his park the Palace Park of America, Lucas moved the NL entry to new grounds at Vandeventer and Natural Bridge avenues where Beaumont High School now stands. The park was then known as Union Park or, variously, Union Grounds. The first NL game was played there on April 30, 1885, with St. Louis beating Chicago 3–2.

Meanwhile, the Browns, after slipping to fourth in the AA in 1884, developed as the powerhouse of their league under the field leadership of young Charlie Comiskey. They won AA pennants in 1885, 1886, 1887, and 1888 with Chris Van der Ahe loudly proclaiming himself the genius of the baseball world. The Browns became an almost annual entrant in the postseason World Series with the NL. They fought to a draw in 1885 with Cap Anson's Cubs, each team winning three games and one ending in a tie. In 1886 St. Louis rocked the NL by beating Chicago four games to two. But the next two Series resulted in losses to Detroit in 1887 and the New York Giants, 6–4, in 1888. So infuriated was genius Van der Ahe that he fired Comiskey and sold most of his stars. Brooklyn won the AA title in 1889 using most of the former St. Louis players, and Comiskey was rehired.

Lucas, however, was not having as much good fortune with his Maroons. After terrorizing the UA, they found the going much tougher in the NL. The competition with the Browns was too much, and the Maroons left the NL after two seasons, leaving the AA in command of the city.

Unable to regain their championship form, the Browns managed to finish second, third, and second in the last three seasons of the AA and when the league folded, Van der Ahe got an NL franchise. In his desperate attempts to maintain the profitability of his team, Van der Ahe had turned Sportsman's Park into a racetrack, incurring the wrath of Spink and other local newspapermen. It also didn't do the park any good. So Van der Ahe moved his NL team to Lucas's old park at Vandeventer and Natural Bridge for the 1892 season.

With Comiskey now managing at Cincinnati, Van der Ahe was no longer a genius. He also had other problems. He was continually rebuilding his park, which had been struck by fire six times in ten years. He attempted to glorify it by building "tall, majestic" iron columns placed behind the stands so as not to interfere with the fans' view of the game. In 1898 Van der Ahe was succeeded by Benjamin S. Muckenfuss as president of the club, and the flamboyant German-accented beer garden proprietor faded from the baseball scene.

Now known as League Park, the Vandeventer lot was soon to acquire its permanent name of Robison Field.

The Robison brothers, who owned the Cleveland club in the NL, got control of St. Louis as well in 1899. They decided to shift their best players from Cleveland to St. Louis and consolidate them into one strong team. This finished Cleveland but saved St. Louis when the NL cut down to eight teams from twelve after the 1899 season.

In 1902 St. Louis was to become a two-team city again, and Sportsman's Park was once again to serve as home for a big league team. The new American League switched its Milwaukee franchise that year, and again a baseball war flared in St. Louis. Newly outfitted in red by the Robisons, the NL club became known as the Cardinals and remained in Robison Field until 1920, when Branch Rickey finally disposed of it and moved the team to Sportsman's Park. Rickey's relationship with the Browns, whom he formerly managed, was vital in enabling the NL to escape from its wooden home at Vandeventer and Natural Bridge, closing the last wooden park in the majors on June 6, 1920, as the Cardinals beat the Cubs 5–2.

Sportsman's Park

When Ralph T. Orthwein agreed to take over a St. Louis club for Ban Johnson in the American League, he was naturally guided to the old Grand Avenue site. Sportsman's Park was in need of some renovation, but it was easier to accomplish that work on short notice than build anew.

After two seasons as president, Orthwein sold the Browns to Robert Lee Hedges. Hedges was to make the first important changes in the stands at Sportsman's Park since the AA days when it was a single-deck stand with a roof covering the seats behind the plate from first base to third. After the 1908 season, Hedges erected a permanent double-deck stand from first to third with pavilions adjacent to the grandstand and bleachers in the outfield. His rebuilding included the introduction of concrete and steel in the main stand. When the new stands were first used on April 14, 1909, they were only the second of their type in the majors, although the

Sportsmans Park, used for nearly a century by various baseball clubs, became a concrete park in 1909 and later served as a joint home for two clubs (Browns and Cardinals) for thirty-three seasons, longer than any other similar arrangement. (*Photo here and on page 208 courtesy of St. Louis Cardinals*)

Daffy Dean is on the mound for the Cardinals in the 1934 World Series against Detroit at Sportsman Park in St. Louis. Former owner Robert Hedges's original concrete grandstand served as part of the park until its abandonment in early 1966. (*Photo courtesy UPI*)

building was not a new structure. Hedges's new Sportsman's Park had a capacity of 18,500.

In 1914 the Federal League war began, and Phil Ball was the owner of the St. Louis club. He proved to be a tough adversary. Neither of the St. Louis clubs was particularly strong, and when the FL fight ended Ball was to purchase the Browns as part of the peace settlement. He controlled the club and Sportsman's Park until his death in 1933. Ball agreed to permit the Cardinals to play there in 1920, the return of the NL coming on July 1. After gaining such stars as Ken Williams and George Sisler, the Browns began to draw greater attendance—especially after the near miss in the 1922 AL pennant race.

So Ball decided to expand Sportsman's Park. Following the 1925 season he extended the double-deck grandstand into the left and right corners and put a roof on the right-field pavilion. His $500,000 job nearly doubled the capacity of the park, increasing it to 30,000. The work also extended the right-field corner distance from 315 feet to 320 and the left-field line from 340 to 355. For the 1926 season, center field was 430 feet from the plate.

After Ball's death, Sportsman's Park became the property of the Dodier Real Estate Company. It returned to the direct control of the Browns in 1946 when Richard C. Muckerman, who bought the team from Don Barnes in 1945, acquired it. Barnes had despaired of making the Browns show a profit and had sought to move the team. A meeting was set in Chicago for December 8, 1941, to vote on the transfer to Los Angeles. When the league officials arrived and saw the headlines announcing Pearl Harbor, it was obvious the Browns were remaining in St. Louis; wartime travel restrictions were likely to make West Coast trips impossible.

The Browns were ultimately acquired by Bill Veeck, who introduced some of the most famous hijinks in baseball records to Sportsman's Park, including the appearance of the famous midget batter, Eddie Gaedel, against Detroit, and the use of contortionist Max Patkin as a first base coach.

In 1944 the Browns won their only pennant in St. Louis, crawling home ahead of a field of war-time teams stripped of their stars. That year they drew 508,644.

In 1946 they attracted 526,435. But almost since the day they moved into Sportsman's Park as tenants, the Cardinals had become the dominant team in St. Louis. In 1933, the year of Phil Ball's death, the Browns failed to draw even 100,000 fans. But they couldn't dispossess the Cards because the rent was a crucial factor in their revenue situation. Thus, the Browns were entrapped by their own ballpark.

Veeck jacked the attendance up to 518,796 in 1952 with his merriment, almost double the figure for the prior year. But the Browns were still in deep trouble. On April 9, 1953, Veeck solved part of his cash problem by selling the park to August Busch, the new owner of the Cardinals, for $800,000 and leasing it back for five years at $175,000 per season. The next day its new owner changed the name of the park to Busch Stadium.

But the Browns stumbled through another horrid season and drew only 297,238 into their games. Veeck, who was frustrated by the other AL owners in his attempts to move the club, finally sold it to a Baltimore group who shifted the Browns to that city for 1954. Since Phil Ball's death in 1933, only minor changes in the press box, concession stands, and elevator facilities had been made in Sportsman's Park. Gussie Busch changed that. He spent $1,500,000 over the winter of 1953 to 1954 to rehabilitate the park, installing new box seats, renovating the clubhouses and dugouts, and making other widespread improvements in the building. Sportsman's Park, as Busch Stadium, was ready for the final phase of its existence. Its final dimensions were 310 feet to right, 422 to center, and 351 to left.

The Cardinals won their first pennant ever in 1926 and promptly beat the Yankees in a seven-game World Series that featured Grover Cleveland Alexander striking out Tony Lazzeri with the bases loaded in the seventh inning of the final game in New York. They added more flags in 1928, 1930, 1931, and 1934 with the famous "Gashouse Gang," which included, at various times, such stars as Rogers Hornsby, Frankie Frisch, Pepper Martin, and the pitching Dean brothers, Dizzy and Paul.

A new crew of Cardinals stars produced by the Rickey farm system—including Mort and Walker Cooper, the brother battery; Whitey Kurowski; Marty Marion; Enos (Country) Slaughter; and all-time great Stan (the Man) Musial—hung up a new string of Cardinal championships starting in 1942. Having won the World Series in 1931 and 1934, the Cardinals captured the third straight Series in which they participated in 1942. They then won flags in 1943 and 1944, beating their landlords, the Browns, in the 1944 Series; and 1946, when they defeated Boston and Ted Williams.

In 1964 it was Bob Gibson's strong-arm pitching, along with the work of Ken Boyer, Curt Flood, Tim McCarver, and Lou Brock, which made the Cardinals NL champions for the tenth time. They faced the Yankees again in the Series and after a seesaw struggle came down to the seventh game at St. Louis on October 15. Gibson, making his second start in three days, grimly hung on for a 7–5 victory over Yankee rookie Mel Stottlemyre, and the Cardinals were World Champions again. It was the final series game ever played at Busch Stadium.

Two years later, in early 1966, the history of the park, which began in 1871, came to a close.

Busch Memorial Stadium

Marking its tenth season of usage in 1975, Busch Memorial Stadium in the heart of the St. Louis Civic Center complex is more than a little unusual among the superstadiums of the 1970s. Since the first Cardinal game on May 12, 1966, the Busch Memorial Stadium has become the focal point of a private-capital project that has generated over $1,500,000 in revenue for the city of St. Louis in lieu of taxes and has paid all of its own expenses at the same time.

The 50,126-seat ballpark is one of eleven developed pieces of property on the Civic Center Redevelopment Corporation real estate located on the Mississippi River waterfront adjacent to the symbolic Archway. Other properties in the complex generate revenue that is normally sufficient to erase the debt incurred by the Stadium operations. Citing 1972 as an example, the Civic Center Redevelopment Corporation indicates that Busch Memorial Stadium lost $409,491 in net cash flow

terms, but the deficit was covered by income from the other properties.

The completely enclosed circular ballpark has its playing field some 12 to 28 feet below the surface of the surrounding street level, and its roof towers 130 feet above the field. For the statistically inclined, Busch Memorial Stadium covers 30.3 acres, rests on a foundation supported by over fifty miles of 11-inch and 14-inch piping down to cement-filled bedrock, and the playing field itself covers 141,500 square feet.

Among the features of the ballpark are 312 deluxe boxes, each containing eight seats and available seasonally for $4,500 per box. Like all of its contemporaries, Busch Memorial Stadium contains a large proportion of box seats, including 11,985 in the lower level and 2,646 in the upper level. Nearly 70 percent of its seats are under cover and about 30 percent of them are below the street-level entrance of which there are nine. Though originally built with a natural grass diamond, Busch Memorial was converted to AstroTurf in 1970.

Among the more interesting features of the Stadium is the St. Louis Sports Hall of Fame, which is located between gates five and six and is open daily from 10:00 A.M. to 5:00 P.M. as well as nights of Cardinal games until 11:00 P.M. Included in this area is a general sports history of the St. Louis area including early baseball fields, teams, and players, an outstanding collection of trophies and mementos from the Cardinals and the Browns, an entire area devoted to Stan Musial and his career, and a fabulous model of old Sportsman's Park. The model is composed of 15,000 pieces and is built on the scale of one-eighth inch per foot.

The Cardinals continued to make some history in their new ballpark, winning NL pennants in 1967 and 1968 under the field leadership of Red Schoendienst, a long-time teammate of Musial's on the Cardinals' championship clubs of the 1940s.

Busch Memorial Stadium is slightly more traditional in its concept as a ballpark and gets high marks for nostalgia in its Hall of Fame, which also covers sports other than baseball.

Busch Memorial Stadium is unique in its ownership. A civic private corporation operates it and several surrounding buildings, producing revenue for the city. The Cardinals set new club attendance records after moving into the stadium in 1966. (*Photo here and page 211 courtesy of St. Louis Cardinals*)

San Diego

Down in the Mission Valley is a place where a fan used to be able to catch up on his sleep and not be bothered with a lot of noisy company. But in 1974 a new owner, some new players, and a few breaks perked things up at San Diego Stadium. Hitting one million paid admissions for the first time that year, a lot of baseball fans in the San Diego area found out how to get to the ballpark. For those who didn't know or who hadn't watched San Diego baseball since the Pacific Coast League played in old Lane Field, the route is Friar's Road.

Built in 1967, San Diego Stadium was without a baseball tenant until the National League expansion of 1969 placed the Padres, who adopted the old PCL nickname, in the park. Prior to the Padres' arrival, the ballpark was used for some exhibition games, the first being a matchup between the Cleveland Indians and the San Francisco Giants on April 5, 1968.

The first official major league game in San Diego was played on the night of April 8, 1969, when the Padres squeezed past Houston 2–1. But despite all of the efforts of Buzzy Bavasi and his front office staff, the Padres progressed slowly and drew about the same. The first Padre season produced 512,970 paid admissions, the second 643,679. Of the next three, only one exceeded the 1970 figure and that by about 600 fans. In 1971 the Padres earned the dubious distinction of being the only NL club not to draw at least one million fans. But all of that changed in 1974, and the pretty San Diego Stadium abounded with fans.

The 1974 attendance surge was such that it wiped

(Photo courtesy of San Diego Padres)

214

out the previous club records for attendance on opening day, a single day game, a day doubleheader, and a single night game plus the club season record.

San Diego Stadium was constructed following the approval by local voters of a 27-million-dollar bond issue and is administered by a nine-man commission. The stadium is reasonably good for viewing baseball, partly because it is on the small side (47,634 seats) and partly because of its rather odd shape. The ballpark looks like a box with only three sides. The stands extend down the first and third base lines and into left field, but the right-field area is open. There is a small bleacher section in right and the large scoreboard sits on pillars behind it.

The stadium is another of those which has its playing field below grade level. Entrance is through tunnel-type gates on all four sides and then upward through one of six coil-shaped towers which are located two on each of the completed sides.

Except for the small open stand in right, San Diego Stadium is essentially a five-level ballpark with 6,394 boxes on the lower level, 8,183 reserved seats on the next level, 1,918 press level boxes, 11,224 upper boxes, and 19,915 general admission seats.

Its playing field is 330 feet down each line, 375 in right and left center, and 420 to straightaway center. The walls are 17 feet high in right and left with a 10-foot fence running from right center to left center.

Like its NL neighbor to the north, Dodger Stadium, the San Diego ballpark benefits from its surroundings. Sunsets in Southern California make a great backdrop for batting practice in addition to reflecting hues off of hills.

But for all of it, San Diego Stadium and the Padres owe their increase in attendance and attention to the involvement of new owner Ray Kroc more than anything else. Kroc, boss man of the MacDonald's fast food chain, made what seemed to be an unfortunate public address announcement, saying, in essence, that the fans deserved better for their money, after a rather poor Padre performance in early 1974. The resulting furor proved, above all, one thing. Kroc, the club's chief owner, cared about the team and how it performed. The fans and players both responded to that outburst in positive ways. San Diego now looks like a healthier outpost for big league baseball than it has at anytime since the NL moved into San Diego Stadium in 1969.

San Francisco

Baghdad by the Bay, romantic San Francisco, rhapsodized in song and story. . . . The lure of rolling hills, clanging cable cars, and glib Mayor George Christopher drew Horace Stoneham and his New York Giants west to fabled San Francisco after the 1957 season. They got some help from the promise of pay television riches and the fact that the Dodgers had already announced a switch from Brooklyn to Los Angeles.

Once they arrived, the Giants were greeted with tumultuous welcomes, enthusiastic crowds, and near-capacity at every game in their temporary home at Seals Stadium. For two years, while their new Taj Mahal was under construction at Candlestick Point, the Giants played in the former home of the Pacific Coast League Seals at 16th and Bryant streets near downtown San Francisco.

This cozy little park had a capacity of 22,900 and in their two seasons there, the Giants drew 2,694,755. This was some 587,000 more than they had attracted in their last *three* seasons in New York in a ballpark that held 56,000. Seals Stadium was certainly a familiar locale for Bay Area baseball fans. In 1946 the PCL Seals, managed by Frank O'Doul, won the pennant and the postseason playoffs. While the team was achieving its laurels, the fans were clicking through the gates at a rate that produced 670,563 paid admissions by season's end. The Seals were historically a strong PCL team, either winning or sharing fourteen pennants or playoff championships. They finished with a flag in 1957, their final season before making way for the Giants.

Seal Stadium's dimensions were also comfortable for major league hitters. The field measured 340 feet to left, 400 to center, and 365 to right. Center field presented a bit of a problem because of the thirty foot high wall that cut across from right center to left center. But hitters, for the most part, could just level on anything good and have confidence in hitting the ball where it was pitched.

The enthusiasm was contagious. The Giants had drifted home in sixth place during the 1957 race while they were based in New York. With the infusion of some new blood from the minor leagues and a healthy dose of local interest, reflected in an almost double attendance in 1958 at San Francisco, the club rose to third.

Mayor Christopher made good on his promise in 1960 when the workmen of the Charles Harney Construction Company completed Candlestick Park. The Giants moved into their Bayshore base with its 45,774 seats and immediately set an all-time club attendance record of 1,795,356 in 1960.

In 1961 San Francisco played host to a major league All-Star Game for the first time and put Candlestick Park on national television. It was a revealing experience for fans in the rest of the nation. Located as it is and built as it was, Candlestick Park proved to be a veritable wind tunnel which gleefully gathered gusts and, particularly late in the afternoon or early in the evening, made them a pivotal part of the game.

The All-Star Game in 1961, the first of two that year, became famous thanks to the wild winds. In the ninth, Stu Miller came on in relief and was literally blown off the mound. In the process, he committed a costly balk.

Seals Stadium was one of the minors' most famous parks and the home of PCL clubs that set attendance records. All those records were smashed when the Giants moved from New York and used the park for two seasons. New left-field bleachers were added for the Giants' NL games. Note the absence of a warning track around the outfield. (*Photo courtesy of UPI*)

The whirling winds led to a throwing error by Ken Boyer in the tenth, which gave the visiting Americans a brief lead. Fortunately for the home team, two singles wrapped around a double by hometown hero Willie Mays gave the Nationals two in the last of the tenth and a 5–4 victory marred by seven errors, the balk, and the wind.

The Giants, of course, had become aware of the wind problems long before the television viewers. In addition to blowing balls in odd directions, the wind also knocked the usually chilly San Francisco temperatures down even further than normal. A heating system was installed for the fans to encourage them to attend night games. The Giants' program for years carried a line warning that the club made no warranty as to the effectiveness of the Candlestick Park heating system. The reason for this was it didn't work very well.

Stoneham had never been inclined to play a heavy night-game schedule. This was fortunate because in San Francisco many day games outdrew night games because of the cold. The Giants still play fewer night games than almost any club in the NL (except Chicago, of course) and the two basic reasons for this are Stoneham's personal traditional feeling and the cold wind which can drive the temperature down twenty degrees during the course of a game.

Another effect of the wind was that balls hit into left center died long before they reached the fence. Although built as a symmetrical park, Candlestick shortly became very unsymmetrical when the fence was drawn in from the left-field corner into the power alley to, in effect, equalize the distance and compensate for the wind currents.

Hitters have their own ways of compensating. The right-handed sluggers like Willie Mays and Orlando Cepeda began to lay back and wait for the high outside pitch that they could ride into the air in right center. There, it took advantage of what amounted to a tail wind which drove it right out of the park. The wind, blowing in from left, curled around the stands and blew outward again toward right center.

In 1970 work began on rebuilding Candlestick Park. This was primarily intended to move the local pro football club into the park, but it had its fallout on the Giants as well. The stands were enclosed all the way around the park, giving it an elliptical shape. The wind factor was reduced, though not completely eliminated. The field, which had been natural grass since 1960, was

Candlestick Park as it originally looked after its openings in 1960 (opposite page). The playing field was natural grass and the park was open in the outfield. Its famous winds caused fences inside the park to be altered in an effort to restore the balance between right- and left-field homer targets. (*Photo above and lower right courtesy of UPI; photo upper right courtesy of Harry M. Stevens & Co.*)

Enclosed to provide additional seating for pro football, Candlestick Park today is the largest capacity ballpark in the NL. AstroTurf is now used on the playing field; doubledecking the stands reduced the wind factor somewhat. The park still has many local critics. (*Photos courtesy of UPI*)

ripped up and replaced with AstroTurf. The seating capacity was expanded to 59,091 for baseball, making Candlestick Park the largest park in the National League.

At the same time, however, things were going downhill for the Giants. An ugly public squabble broke out between the city and the club over the method of paying for the expansion of Candlestick. The argument revolved around a surcharge on baseball tickets. The arrival of the A's in Oakland cut deeply into the Giants' base for attendance. Since 1968, the first AL year in Oakland, the Giants have drawn over one million only once, and that was in 1971 when they won the West Division title in a wild race. In 1974 their attendance

(Scorecard from Shannon Collection)

dipped to a low of 520,081, fewer than had been drawn by a Giant club—in New York or San Francisco—since 1943. The irony of a 33 percent increase in park capacity while attendance was dropping to all-time lows struck a sour note on all sides.

But the Giants have had their moments of glory in Candlestick, too. The most successful season on the field came in 1962 when they roared to the NL pennant, defeating the arch-rival Dodgers in a three-game playoff for the flag. They then carried the Yankees to seven games in the World Series. One of Candlestick's most memorable moments came in that seventh game on October 16, 1962. Ralph Terry, victim of Bill Mazeroski's classic homer in the ninth inning of the 1960 seventh game, was on the mound for the Yankees. The Series, which had begun in San Francisco on October 4, had struggled through rain on both coasts for the best part of two weeks as the teams split the first six games.

Now the climax was at hand. In the ninth, the Giants trailed 1–0, and with two outs put two men on the bases. The tying run was at third, and Mays was at second with a potential run which meant the game and the Series if he could get home. Ralph Houk, the Yankee manager, elected to pitch to terrifying Willie McCovey. McCovey ripped a Terry pitch like a bullet toward right center. Yankee second baseman Bobby Richardson, who appeared to struggle to keep his feet from the force of the drive, grabbed the ball and hung on to end the Series and give the Yankees the championship.

During the first eight years the park operated, Giant attendance averaged 1,537,506. But the steep decline since 1968 has raised many questions about the Giants and their park. In fifteen seasons, 17,859,650 fans have watched regular-season NL games at Candlestick Park. How many more will be afforded the privilege remains, at present, an open question. But for all of the travail, Candlestick Park remains as unique as its environment.

224

Seattle

On April 11, 1969, Seattle, the twenty-second largest city in the nation with a metropolitan area of 1.5 million, joined the major leagues. It was a day of considerable, but not overwhelming, excitement in Seattle.

A big-league ballgame was being played for the first time in Sicks' Stadium, the 25,420-seat ballpark on South Rainier Avenue that had been the home for decades of Pacific Coast League teams. But only 14,993 fans turned out to watch the new Seattle Pilots whip Chicago in the opener.

Sicks' Stadium, the third former PCL park to be used for major league baseball (the earlier ones were Seals Stadium in 1958 and Wrigley Field in Los Angeles in 1961), was named for Emil Sick, long-time owner of the PCL Seattle Rainiers.

The new American League club was owned by Bill Daley, formerly a part-owner of the Cleveland Indians, and two well-known brothers in baseball, Max and Dewey Soriano. It had been named after a contest in which a local man suggested that Pilots were indicative of Seattle's leadership in both marine and air activities. Aircraft plants form a vital part of the Seattle area economy.

Undaunted by the seeming lack of blazing interest among local fans, the pristine Pilots knocked off Chicago for a second straight day on April 12. But it was too good to be true. Turning major league hitters loose in a park like Sicks' Stadium, you just had to expect some fireworks.

The siege guns made their first real appearance on April 13, when five different White Sox batters hit a homer apiece as Chicago finally beat the Pilots 12–7. From then on, it was an average of almost two homers a game all season long.

The construction of Sicks' Stadium was in the old style in several ways. It was a single-deck affair with a roof over the stands behind the plate between first base and third base. The press box was cut into the roof directly behind the plate with a small deck for cameramen underneath. Mounted on top of the roof were four of the ballpark's light towers, although bright lights were not one of the strong features of Sicks' Stadium.

The outfield was surrounded by small bleachers that were packed into the plot of the park at the expense of outfield territory. Down the line in left the park measured 305 feet, breaking out slightly to 345 in the power alley. In right field it was 320 down the line and 345 into right center. Straightaway center field was 405 feet. Despite the generally rainy climate, the ballpark's chummy confines made it appealing to AL hitters who collected 167 homers in Sicks' Stadium during its only season in the league.

Of the 167 homers at Seattle, the Pilots got only seventy-four and the visiting clubs ninety-three. Oakland led the parade with thirteen as a team, Chicago hit eleven as did Baltimore, and Cleveland hitters collected ten.

Certain players, of course, did better than others. Called up to the Pilots late in the season from the minors, former Met Greg Goosen found Sicks' Stadium just to his liking. He hit ten homers during that partial season, all of them in Seattle.

Sicks' Stadium head groundskeeper Elmer Driver reads a newspaper report about a new domed stadium in Seattle. By the time it was finally built, the AL club had long before moved to Milwaukee. The inadequacy of Sicks' Stadium, formerly a PCL park, was one of the reasons cited for the move. (*Photo courtesy of UPI*)

General manager Marvin Milkes had set third place as his goal for the expansion Pilots. This lofty aim was almost realized. In fact, the club did get that high during midseason, but a rash of injuries and the recurring military obligations of Mike Hegan, a .292 hitter at season's end, crippled the team and it sank to sixth at the close of the race. Manager Joe Schultz was fired and replaced by Dave Bristol. But the real struggle in Seattle had only just begun.

The club had produced some decent ballplayers for an expansion team, including pitcher Gene Brabender, who won more games (thirteen) that season than any pitcher had ever won for a first-year expansion club.

Attendance had been fairly strong until August. After a crowd of 23,657 nearly filled Sicks' Stadium to watch the Yankees beat the Pilots 5–3, the fans did a vanishing act. The team's continued injuries were a factor, but the owners felt it was only a partial one. For a first-year team, the attendance in so large a market was disappointing.

Low gate receipts coupled with a lack of local television revenue made for a difficult cash picture. Then a bank loan was called, and the club was for sale. Daley and his associates sought local buyers but could find none who met with AL approval, and the club was sold to Milwaukee interests and moved to the Wisconsin city. Litigation over the move followed and remains.

For old Sicks' Stadium, the moment in the sun was a brief one and perhaps not as enjoyable as it should have been. But a lot of hitters got to add Sicks' to their list of parks in which they hit homeruns.

The departure of the Pilots for Milwaukee, where they became the Brewers, left one of the most impressive ballparks of the future without a team. Voters in the Seattle area approved a bond issue for the construction of a King County Domed Stadium near the Seattle Center after the expansion of the AL voted in 1967 produced a franchise for Seattle. Construction on the domed stadium continues and it is expected to be completed in 1975. But it will open without one of the staple elements of ballpark operation—a ballclub.

Meanwhile, Seattle officials continue to search for a baseball tenant for the new stadium, hoping for a transfer of an existing team or the possibility of another expansion by one of the major leagues. What effect the continuing litigation against the AL will have on this prospect is not clear. But the new domed stadium will join the New Orleans Superdome as an inviting ballpark for any major league club that may not be prospering.

Built in 1938, Sicks' Stadium was originally called Sicks' Select Stadium, after owner Emil Sicks' local beer. The PCL Rainiers played there until 1969 when the AL Pilots used the park for one season. (*Photo from the Shannon Collection*)

Texas

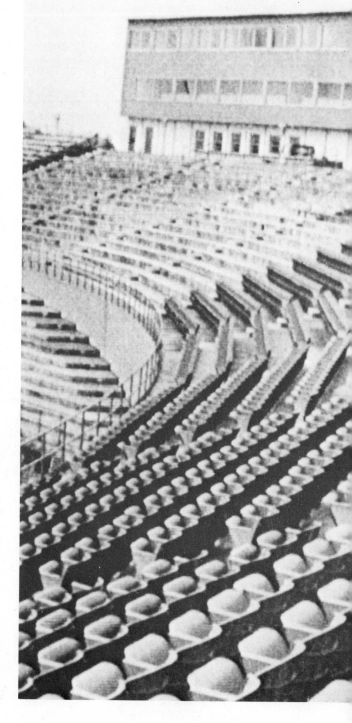

When the Texas Rangers first appeared in 1972, they had two prime assets: Frank Howard and Ted Williams. At the end of the first season, both were gone. Yet the 1972 season achieved something that might have seemed hard to believe even a year before. It put Arlington, Texas, in the major leagues.

When originally constructed as Turnpike Stadium in 1965, Arlington Stadium was designed to serve as the home of a Texas League club with the hope that the next expansion of the major leagues would bring a franchise to the Dallas-Fort Worth area. Arlington is situated almost exactly between the two major Texas cities.

Both major leagues did, in fact, expand in 1969, and the new franchises went to Seattle, Kansas City, Montreal, and San Diego.

But the financial difficulties of Bob Short, owner of the Washington Senators, and his running feud with his landlord at Robert F. Kennedy Stadium, the District of Columbia Armory Board, finally gave a new ray of hope to the baseball fans in the Arlington area. That hope was fulfilled when Short agreed to move his team into Turnpike Stadium and rename them the Texas Rangers.

Once their creation was achieved, the Rangers weren't going to get off on schedule. The 1972 season was delayed by the first baseball players' strike in modern history. Big league baseball finally came to Arlington on April 21. A crowd of 20,105 turned out to watch the new Rangers beat California 7–6, with Dick Bosman besting Clyde Wright.

But Texans, though enthusiastic, are also sophisticated. The next day's game drew only 5,517 in good

After Arlington Mayor Tom Vandergriff persuaded the Senators to move from Washington and become the Texas Rangers, Turnpike Stadium was expanded into Arlington Stadium and then-Senator manager Ted Williams came down to take a look around the new ballpark. (*Photo above courtesy of UPI; photos pages 230 and 231 courtesy of Texas Rangers*)

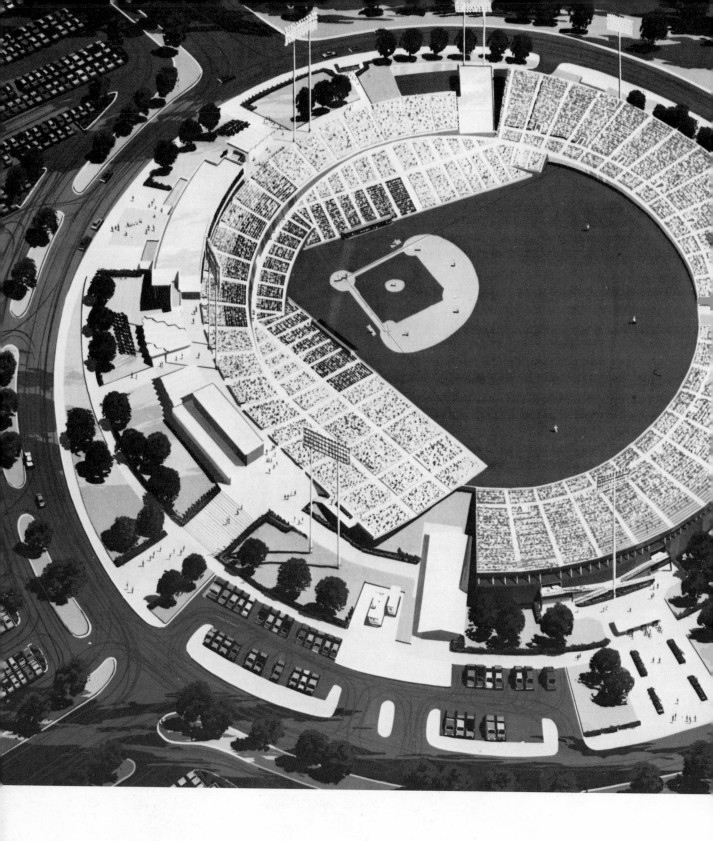

weather. The disruption caused by the players' strike notwithstanding, the fans wanted to wait and see what happened with the team on the field.

When they found out that the Rangers really were just the old Senators in new clothes, the attendance dropped sharply and finished the season at 662,974, just a shade ahead of the previous season in Washington. In 1973 it rose slightly to 686,152 despite the fact that Williams, one of baseball's great names, was no longer the field manager and Howard, the best known of the original Rangers, had gone off to Japan via Detroit.

But in 1974 the Ranger fans came to life largely because the team did. New manager Billy Martin sparked the club into the West Division pennant race and the attendance shot up to 1,193,903, fourth highest in the American League and nearly equal to the total of the first two seasons at Arlington Stadium.

Since shortly after the start of the 1974 season, the Texas Rangers have been owned by a local syndicate. Dr. Bobby Brown, the former Yankee, served as club president for 1974 but stepped down after the season ended to return to his medical activities.

The park which contained all of this enthusiasm is the second smallest in the American League (ahead of only Boston's Fenway Park) and third smallest in the majors (Montreal's Jarry Park is the major league midget with 28,000 seats). Arlington Stadium has 35,698 seats, more than half of them general admission seats in the terrace. The box and reserved seats in the park are the molded plastic type now becoming popular in the new ballparks. They fill what is a single-deck park in essentially two levels. The entranceways are at the midpoint of the stadium with one level, mainly boxes, located below grade level. Somewhat like Anaheim Stadium, only more so, Arlington Stadium has a massive amusement park as a neighbor. Six Flags Over Texas, one of the principal tourist attractions in the Dallas-Fort Worth area, is located immediately adjacent to Arlington Stadium. Both facilities use electric tram cars to transport their patrons from the large parking lots that surround them.

Arlington Stadium is built in a convex manner so that the top rows of seats in the park extend over the lower portions of the park's exterior. Although it is a small park, it does not give the feeling of intimacy usually associated with small-capacity ballparks. It has a large, open-air feeling imparted to an extent by the vastness of the Texas skies, which seem to run uninterrupted for miles in all directions. Nothing actually encloses or confines the area in which the park is situated; no massive buildings or office towers give relativity to its size.

One of the dominating features of Arlington Stadium is its scoreboard, which is shaped like the state of Texas. This novel configuration gives the entire park something of its character. The motif is carried through in the uniforms of the usherettes and vendors. Beer is sold out of plastic buckets filled with ice, and as a result Arlington Stadium is one of the parks in the majors where the vendor's cry of "cold beer" is really meaningful.

Arlington Stadium presents decent targets for hitters in its symmetrical playing dimensions. It is 330 feet down each line, 370 into the power alleys, and an even 400 feet to straightaway center. While the outfield fence is only 11 feet high, the hitter seeking a real challenge can try to hit one completely out of the stadium into the Texas air. Clearing the stands down the lines would require a blast of 443 feet or, if something bigger is desired, a ball striking the base of the scoreboard would have to travel 512 feet. For a real Texas-style wallop, a homer that clears the center-field stands would have to go 541 feet.

Given the generally hot weather in the area, Texas is the park in the AL that logs the most night action. In 1974 only four afternoon games were on the schedule after opening day plus one 5:00 P.M. start and three 6:00 P.M. twilight games. Even the Sunday games are generally played at night—the only park in the majors where this is a standard procedure.

Washington, D.C.

The early ballpark history of Washington begins and ends with one man, Michael Scanlon. Scanlon, a combination pool-room operator and promoter of sports events, was also an expert on baseball, its rules, and its players. He nurtured a long-time dream of seeing Washington in a big league. For Mike Scanlon the dream was to ultimately come true, but only after severe bumps along the way.

Washington's first baseball clubs, the Olympics and the Nationals, were formed in 1859. Although slightly younger, the Nationals were to achieve the greater fame in the early days of organized baseball. Many of the games involving those teams were played on the White Lot, an open park behind the grounds of the Executive Mansion, now better known as the White House.

Mike Scanlon built the first enclosed ballpark in Washington. In 1870 he opened a small wooden park near 17th and S streets, N.W. It contained 500 seats and Scanlon charged 25 cents for admission. The next year, the National Association became the first organized league, and Scanlon was thrilled to see the Olympics as entrants in the circuit. In 1872 the Nationals also joined the NA. By 1873 the league was already starting to fall apart, and the Nationals dropped out early in the year. The Olympics also quit before the season was over, and Washington was again in baseball limbo. When the National League was organized in 1876, it didn't bother to place a club in Washington.

Scanlon continued his efforts to arouse interest in the game with a dogged persistence. In 1884 both the outlaw Union Association and the established American Association placed teams in the national capital. The AA club was placed there largely as a counter to the UA team. It showed some promise by winning its opening game on May 1, routing Brooklyn 12–0. But the promise was short-lived and Washington was out of the AA at the end of the season. Since the UA folded after that first season, Washington was once more without a league club.

The nucleus of the Nationals continued to function, however, and the team picked up a franchise in the Eastern League, a minor circuit on the eastern seaboard, in 1885. To the surprise of many local fans, the club won the Eastern League pennant. Emboldened by this triumph, the Hewitt brothers, Robert and Walter, along with the other chief backers of the club, sought out NL president Nicholas Young. The Hewitts got a NL franchise for 1886.

With the new franchise in the major leagues, the Hewitts set out to build a new park worthy of Washington's new station in baseball life. They leased a plot on North Capitol Avenue between F and G streets, bounded by Delaware Avenue. This land became the site of their park, covering an area 400 feet by 800 feet and leased for a five-year term. The first year rent was $500, rising to $1,000 the second, and $1,250 for each of the last three years. Called Capitol Park, the new field was the first substantial wooden park built in Washington, and had a capacity of 6,000. The club, named the Statesmen, was managed by old standby Mike Scanlon. They won their opener on April 29 over Philadelphia 6–3. But the team didn't fare well, sinking toward its eventual eighth place finish, and old Mike Scanlon was fired on August 20. Subsequent managers in succeeding seasons did little better, achieving seventh, eighth, and eighth place finishes in the next three years. The opening-day crowd in 1886 was the largest up to that time in Washington baseball. But the crowds thereafter were measured by the team's performance, and after the 1889 season the Hewitts were excused from the NL by Young. In 1888, however, the team first became known by the nickname that was to stick with it despite official efforts to change it for decades—the Senators.

After a nonleague season of exhibition games in 1890, Washington again received an AA franchise; but the Association collapsed after the 1891 season, ending that hope.

However, the settlement of the AA withdrawal from competition with the NL brought about the expansion of the National League to twelve clubs. It also precipitated the buying out of the Wagner brothers, George and Jacob Earle, in Philadelphia. Their AA Athletics, one of only four teams to play in each of the AA's ten seasons, was unwelcome in Philadelphia as a rival for the Phillies. But the Wagners were permitted to take a Washington franchise in the expanded NL.

At first viewed as hopeful restorers of the Washington

baseball situation, the brothers soon proved to be something less. But at the outset they established a board of directors made up of local baseball personalities and were influenced by them to build a new park. The new directors, Scanlon among them, suggested a site at The Boundary, where 7th Street N.W. intersected Florida Avenue.

National Park was quickly constructed on the suggested land and opened for business to an overflow crowd of 6,400 on April 16. The new Senators were defeated by the New York Giants 6–5, but the inaugural was considered a success. If it was a success, it was one of the few for the hapless club. The Wagners soon disposed of the local directors and made a career out of peddling their best players to other NL clubs for cash and youngsters. If the young players developed, they, too, were sold. This continuing cycle plagued Washington baseball throughout the Wagner years, which didn't conclude until the contraction of the NL after the 1899 season, when the team was disbanded.

The Wagners showed their true mettle in 1893 when they transferred three home games against Philadelphia to the Phillies' Baker Bowl, where they had drawn a crowd of 15,000 during a previous visit. They shifted three more games to Cleveland for similar reasons.

The 1899 season was the last for Washington in the NL at National Park, but it produced an impressive individual performance. John (Buck) Freeman of the Senators hit twenty-five homeruns to lead the NL and came within two of the league record. He got his twenty-fifth homer in the final NL game ever played in Washington on October 14, 1899.

To insure their departure, the NL paid the Wagners $46,500 for the franchise and the lease on National Park. In 1900 the wooden grandstand was to stand empty. It remained empty in 1901, too, but Washington wasn't without a major league baseball team. The new American League saw to that when it transferred its Kansas City franchise into the nation's capital when war was declared on the NL.

Griffith Stadium

National Park was eventually to become the home of the American League for nearly sixty years. But when the AL first came to town, the rival NL held the lease on the park and was anything but ready to give it to the interlopers.

Jimmy Manning, owner of the Kansas City club the previous season, and Frederick Postal, president of the team in Washington, sought a site for a new ballpark. They found one at 14th Street and Bladensburg, N.E. They slapped together a snug wooden park and called it American League Park. There, AL baseball was introduced to Washington on April 29, 1901. Hungry for action after a year's enforced abstinence, the Washington fans poured out to see the new team. The opening-day crowd was 9,772, including Admiral Dewey, the hero of Manila Bay in the Spanish-American War of 1898. The season attendance was a healthy 358,692 for a team that finished sixth in an eight-club league.

It was at American League Park that the original megaphone man of baseball, E. Lawrence Phillips, got his start announcing lineups to the fans, relieving the umpires of that duty. When he retired in 1928, the practice was universal in baseball.

Flushed by the strong gate, the Senators raised their admission price to seventy-five cents for 1902 and paid the price of greed. The team again came home sixth, but drew only 188,158. After the war with the NL ended, the Senators shifted into National Park with its larger capacity, but they really didn't need the extra seats. In 1911 the old wooden stands caught fire and burned to the ground—except for a few bleachers—while the team was in spring training. Thus, by necessity, the concrete and steel era came to Washington. It came quickly. The single-deck stand from first base to third was built in only eighteen days and opened on schedule.

Early arrivers saw the new park in something of an unfinished state with much of the concrete still clad in wooden forms. All of the seats were uncovered, and no box seats had been installed except for the presidential party. William Howard Taft, a former ballplayer, threw out the ceremonial first ball and became the president who began a custom to be carried forward by all of his successors until Gerald Ford. By the time Mr. Ford became president, the nation's capital no longer had a baseball team.

In 1912 Clark Griffith came to Washington as manager and part owner of the Senators. The ballpark was gradually completed, and by the time the Senators won their first pennant in 1924 it had assumed the shape and capacity it was to maintain throughout its existence as Griffith Stadium. Griffith's prize during his early years in

It's opening day in 1949 at Washington with the Senators facing the Philadelphia Athletics. President Truman threw out the first ball, and Eddie Joost started the game with a fly to Clyde Vollmer in right. In 1945 the season's closing game (previous page) was delayed while burning gasoline was used to dry the field. (*Photos courtesy UPI*)

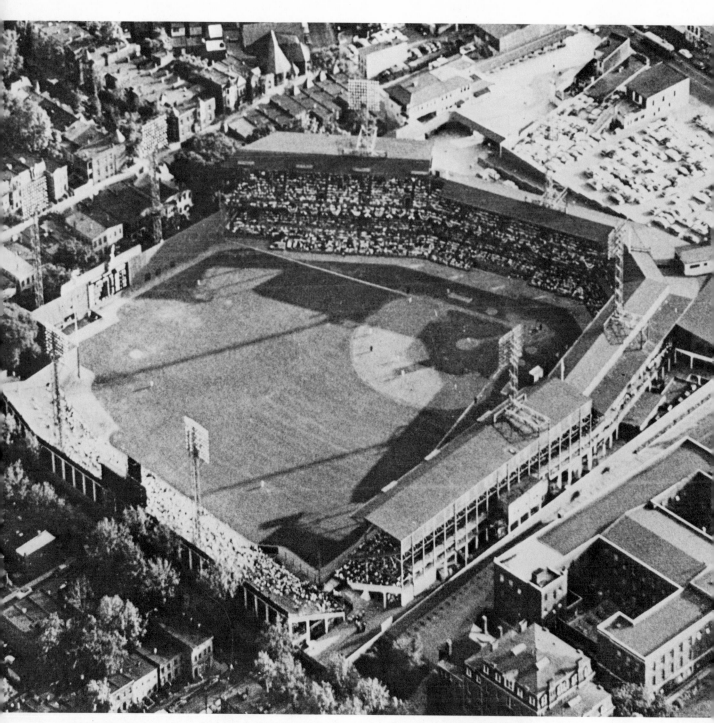

Griffith Stadium, built on the site of old National Park, was used continuously for baseball from 1892 to 1961 except for two seasons. Still, only once during that entire period did a Washington team draw over a million paid admissions in a season. (*Photo above and on page 234 courtesy of UPI*)

Washington was pitching immortal Walter Johnson. Griffith's influence on the development of Griffith Stadium was probably also partly due to his own career as a pitcher of some note.

For whatever reasons, Griffith Stadium was a pitcher's dream. For almost all of its days it measured a staggering 402 feet down the left-field line to the bleachers which crossed into deep left-center. It was 421 to dead center and 328 down the right-field line. But right field was guarded by a 30-foot high wall that salvaged many a pitching mistake, trimming potential homers down to doubles. Griffith Stadium was traditionally the toughest homerun target in the American League. It was also the league's smallest capacity park, never exceeding 30,000 seats.

One of the peculiar features of Griffith Stadium was the difference in the height of the roof over the stands. The new upper-deck stands added by Griffith after he became president of the team in 1920 were covered by a roof that stood considerably higher than the one that covered the original double-deck stands behind the plate. After the new stands were completed, they suddenly came in handy.

In 1924 Griffith named his twenty-four-year-old infielder, Stanley (Bucky) Harris, as the team manager. From fourth place the year before, Harris became baseball's boy wonder, leading the Senators to their first pennant in his initial season. Somewhat disbelieving, the Washington fans were slow to support the club and the attendance for the year was 584,310, one of the lowest totals for a pennant-winning club in modern baseball history.

The pennant put the Senators, or Nats (short for Nationals) as headline writers often tagged them, into the World Series against John McGraw's New York Giants. The teams split the first six games and the decisive seventh was played in Griffith Stadium on October 10. It was a twelve-inning thriller won by Walter Johnson in relief and decided by two bad-bounce hits. The Senators scored first, but the Giants got three in the sixth, holding a 3–1 lead into the home eighth. With runners at second and third, Harris bounced one toward eighteen-year-old Freddie Lindstrom at third base. The ball struck a rock and bounded over Lindstrom's head, sending home the tying runs.

The crowd, which included President and Mrs. Calvin Coolidge (she was the fan, not he), prayed for a run by the Nats. Prayers, as much as anything, were responsible for what happened in the home twelfth. Muddy

Reul hit a high pop foul behind the plate. Giant catcher Hank Gowdy stepped on his mask, and the ball dropped. Thus spared, Reul slammed a double. Then Earl McNeely rapped a bouncer toward third. Again the ball hit a pebble, chopped over the luckless Lindstrom's head, carried into left field, and sent Reul in with the winning run in a 4–3 Senator victory. Of the four Series games at Griffith Stadium, three were decided by the same 4–3 score, two of them in twelve innings, and the other game was a heart-stopping 2–1 Washington win in the sixth game.

In 1925 the Senators again won the title, but not the breaks in the Series. They won two of the three games played in Griffith Stadium, but Johnson took the loss in the decisive seventh game at Pittsburgh, 9–7. As defending world champs, the Senators drew 817,199, third best in team history. The Senators won their third (and final) pennant in 1933, losing the Series to the Giants in five games.

Changes in the team's style and the configuration of the ballpark marked the regime of Calvin Griffith, adopted son of Clark Griffith, and new president of the team in 1956. He shortened the fence in left with a screen in front of the stands and signed such long-ball sluggers as Harmon Killebrew, Roy Sievers, and Jim Lemon to hit balls over it. In 1960 the Senators drew 743,404, the most since 1949, the sixth highest total in team history, and an increase of 128,032 over the previous season. At the end of that season, Calvin Griffith announced that the Senators were shifting to Metropolitan Stadium in Bloomington, Minnesota, as the Minnesota Twins.

D.C. Stadium

Ironically, the U.S. Government had begun a new construction project—a ballpark to be built on the banks of the Potomac near the D.C. Armory—when the Senators decided to end their sixty-year stay in Washington.

However, old Griffith Stadium and the new ballpark got simultaneous reprieves when the AL expanded suddenly for the 1961 season, granting new franchises to

Los Angeles and Washington in the first expansion in its history.

The final presidential opener at Griffith Stadium was played on April 10, 1961, when John F. Kennedy was on hand to throw out the first ball and watch the expansion version of the Senators lose to Chicago 4–3. A former hero of the original Senators, Roy Sievers, slammed a 410-foot homer into the center-field bleachers in the second inning for the game's only homer.

The final AL game at Griffith Stadium came on Thursday, September 21, the game the previous night having been rained out and canceled. The crowd of 1,498 was the lowest of the season. The opponents were the Minnesota Twins which, thanks to the schedule-maker, permitted both of the teams that used the venerable park to join in bringing its history to a close.

On April 9, 1961, District of Columbia Stadium opened. It was only the second new ballpark in the AL since 1932 when Cleveland's Municipal Stadium was first used. The switch of the original Senators had brought Metropolitan Stadium into the league the previous year.

The new park, which was later renamed Robert F. Kennedy Stadium, was an enormous departure from its local predecessor in several ways. Its capacity of 45,016 was one obvious difference. Others were its circular double-deck structure completely surrounding the field, and symmetrical dimensions, which were 335 feet down each line and 410 to center. A screen provided the outfield barrier with the bullpens for both clubs behind it. There were no lower stand seats in the outfield, only the upper ones. A huge scoreboard sat on the ground behind the screen in right-center.

D.C. Stadium was constructed by the federal government in its role as the local government of the District of Columbia. The name was changed to Robert F. Kennedy Stadium in 1968. Washington and Seattle remain as the only former big-league cities without teams. (*Photo courtesy UPI*)

This park, much unlike Griffith Stadium, was made for hitters. The complete enclosure of the field made wind a neglible factor, and the balls carried well. When the Senators obtained Frank Howard in a trade with the Dodgers, they had a genuine power threat who was right at home in these surroundings. Howard led the AL in homers in 1968 and 1970 with forty-four each season.

Howard was also a key figure in the stadium's most dramatic baseball moment. The final game to be played by the Senators before their transfer to Arlington, Texas, was September 30, 1971. That night Howard came to bat for perhaps the last time and received a standing ovation from the crowd of 14,460 in the sixth inning. Yankee pitcher Mike Kekich laid a curve right in to Howard, who obliged the crowd by drilling it into the left bullpen, igniting ripples of ecstasy from the fans and a four-run rally that tied the game. Washington eventually took a 7–5 lead into the ninth and got the first two Yankees out. But then the unruly fans, angered by owner Bob Short's decision to move the team, began coming onto the field in numbers beyond the control of the extremely pacific special police. Unable to maintain order, umpire crew chief Jim Honochick ordered the game forfeited at 10:11 P.M., drawing down a sad final curtain on Washington's checkered career in the major leagues.

A husband and wife team, Marti and Ed Robins, paint AL club logos on top of the visiting dugout at Washington's D.C. Stadium. Logos were part of the traditional decoration at the park during the years it was occupied by the second Washington Senator club. (*Photo courtesy UPI*)

242

Index

INDEX